Winning Ways

for Early Childhood Professionals

Being a Supervisor

Winning Ways
for Early Childhood Professionals

Being a Supervisor

Gigi Schweikert

Name: _____

Date: _____

Redleaf Press®
www.redleafpress.org
800-423-8309

Also in the Winning Ways series by Gigi Schweikert
  Being a Professional
  Partnering with Families
  Becoming a Team Player
  Understanding Infants
  Understanding Toddlers and Twos
  Understanding Preschoolers

Published by Redleaf Press
10 Yorkton Court
St. Paul, MN 55117
www.redleafpress.org

First edition 2014
Cover design by Jim Handrigan
Cover photograph by Ben Stapley
Interior design by Erin Kirk New
Artwork on page 6 by Sophia Montieth
Printed in the United States of America

21 20 19 18 17 16 15 14   2 3 4 5 6 7 8 9

Library of Congress Cataloging-in-Publication Data
Schweikert, Gigi, 1962-
  Winning ways for early childhood professionals : being a supervisor / Gigi Schweikert.
     pages cm — (Winning ways series)
   Summary: "This professional development book helps recently promoted classroom teachers transition from guiding young children to supporting and supervising staff members"—Provided by publisher.
   ISBN 978-1-60554-245-4 (pbk.)
   1. School supervision. 2. Early childhood education.   I. Title.
LB2822.6.S39 2013
372.21—dc23
                              2013030907

Printed on acid-free paper

Contents

From the Desk of Gigi Schweikert

Dear Winning Ways Reader
(and Supervisor),

When I was young, I used to play teacher. I would set up my dolls, teddy bear, and stuffed animals in my make-believe classroom and lead them in activities I had invented. But I never imagined myself in the role of supervising other teachers (since that would have meant putting the teddy bear in charge of the activities). At that age, I wasn't aware of all the planning, teamwork, and leadership involved in supervising an early childhood education program. Now that I know what it's like to be a supervisor, I admire these dedicated leaders even more, especially the ones who have led me over the years.

As I took on different supervisory roles throughout my career—lead teacher, assistant director, director, regional manager, vice president, and all the way up to toilet plunger—I realized I still had a lot to learn. Seems like we supervisors are the ones who fish the toys out of the toilet. Most of us become supervisors because we're good at our teaching jobs, but we quickly find out that leading adults is a bit different from leading children. I quickly found that I had to communicate, connect, and delegate in a whole new way—not so different from letting the teddy bear lead the classroom, after all.

Many of the skills we've learned as teachers can help us as we coach the adults on our team. As children's teachers, we want to help children succeed and grow in their abilities. As supervisors of other teachers, our goal is still the same: we want to help adults be successful, to guide them and encourage them, and to model good leadership for them. And, as with anything else, to be good supervisors we have to be willing to adapt and grow in our own roles. That's probably the hardest part of all.

Whether you're considering a leadership role or you're a veteran supervisor, I hope you find it as challenging and as rewarding as I do! What I've learned from my experiences as a supervisor is outlined in *Being a Supervisor* in a simple and approachable way I think you'll find useful, inspiring, and humorous. You can't get any job completed well without the ability to laugh at yourself. After you finish reading *Being a Supervisor*, send me your thoughts and ideas about being a great supervisor to www.gigischweikert.com. I'd love to hear from you.

Children deserve our winning ways,

Introduction

Are You a Supervisor?

Are you aspiring to become a supervisor in early childhood education? Are you the person everyone at work looks to for help and advice? Have you been a supervisor forever? If you answered yes to any of these questions, then this book is for you. Leadership comes in many forms. *Winning Ways for Early Childhood Professionals: Being a Supervisor* is written to help everyone in early childhood education who guides adults and wants to be a more effective and successful leader. And I bet that's you!

What Makes a Supervisor?

There are many factors that help a supervisor in any field. Good supervisors

- Are approachable and accessible
- Genuinely enjoy their work
- Listen and communicate well
- Respond quickly and appropriately to problems or concerns
- Support their team and use individuals' skills well
- Set a positive approach to the team and inspire others
- Have high standards and integrity

Many early childhood professionals who become supervisors find leading other adults a whole new challenge from guiding and teaching children. But here's the good part: as are all early childhood educators, you are already in a leadership role over the children in your care, and supervisors can use those same skills and principles to guide and support their teams. Pretty cool!

USING THE BOOK

Winning Ways for Early Childhood Professionals: Being a Supervisor has eight supervisory concepts that will enhance and improve your leadership skills:

1 Admitting You're the Supervisor

2 Helping Adults Succeed

3 Creating a Culture That Encourages Input and Allows for Mistakes

4 Motivating Adults through Delegation

5 Communicating Consistently and Honestly

6 Following Through

7 Staying Connected

8 Setting the Tone

Throughout, you'll feel encouraged, empowered, and equipped to guide adults with the same heart and expertise with which you guide children.

There are several ways to use the book:

- Read the entire book on your own and become a better supervisor.

- Use the book as a reference guide and read the chapters that specifically target your skill needs.

- Connect with other supervisors and read the book, discussing each chapter as you go or when you have finished the entire book.

- Create an eight-week or eight-session leadership course for supervisors in your program or community. Meet at a regularly scheduled time and use the self-assessment form as a tool to guide your training.

- Use the book to equip early childhood education students in colleges and universities with the confidence they need to work with adults in the field.

Is *Being a Supervisor* Workbook Intended for Group or Individual Use?

Either way works great! You can use *Being a Supervisor* as a training tool with a group or on your own. Either way, read through the appropriate content and then complete the exercises throughout the book and at the end. Jotting down your answers will give you the greatest benefit from the workbook. If you are in a training group, having a written answer to refer to may help you feel more comfortable sharing your thoughts during the meeting in front of other people.

DESIGN

How Is *Being a Supervisor* Workbook Designed for Training?

The workbook is designed so participants will

- Experience active learning by participating in discussions, solving problems, applying new knowledge to their current work situations, and getting reenergized about working in the early childhood field

- Connect current knowledge with the new material and have opportunities to talk about and share common concerns and issues regarding supervision

- Gain practical knowledge and tips to begin using in their programs immediately

How to Use *Being a Supervisor* Workbook in Trainings

You can use this book for a variety of training needs and situations. Here are some examples:

- Group of supervisors from a program
- Administrative team
- Lunch and learn
- Staff meeting
- In-service day
- Partnership of several programs
- Community outreach
- Recruiting tool
- Local conference

being a supervisor

SELF-ASSESSMENT

How Are You Doing at Being a Supervisor?

Take the following assessment to see how you're doing at being a supervisor. Great supervising can look different from person to person, but assessment centers on activities and attitudes common to all supervisors. Be honest with yourself so that you can really assess your skills as a supervisor. Every supervisor has new things to learn. Understanding your current approach to supervising can help you use your strengths and focus on areas for improvement and enhancement.

1 I accept and feel comfortable in my role as supervisor.

Always   Usually   Sometimes   Never

2 I help adults succeed by making my expectations clear and reasonable.

Always   Usually   Sometimes   Never

3 I encourage input from my team and understand that mistakes happen.

Always   Usually   Sometimes   Never

4 I motivate the adults on my team by delegating meaningful tasks.

Always   Usually   Sometimes   Never

5 I communicate information and feedback consistently and honestly to those I supervise.

Always   Usually   Sometimes   Never

6 I follow through on the tasks and priorities I've promised for myself and my team.

Always   Usually   Sometimes   Never

7 I know and connect with each of my employees regularly to give encouragement and to address problems.

Always   Usually   Sometimes   Never

8 I set a positive, approachable tone for the rest of my staff.

Always   Usually   Sometimes   Never

Eight Steps to Being a Supervisor

Refer back to your completed self-assessment form as you explore the eight topic areas for being a supervisor. Whether you are on your own and reading and working at your leisure, or training with a group, you'll gain practical information you can use in the classroom and techniques for developing better interactions and relationships with your staff. Let's get started.

being a supervisor

1

Admit You're the Supervisor

I accept and feel comfortable in my role as supervisor.

- Always

- Usually

- Sometimes

- Never

How Did You Get Here? Why Are You a Supervisor?

Are you wondering, "How did I get here? Why am I the supervisor?" If you're like most of us, you entered this profession to work with children, not necessarily adults. And here you are, a supervisor, responsible for making sure others do what they're supposed to do, making sure others get to work on time, and making sure others work well with children. You're probably thinking, "Hey, that was my job, working with children."

Here's what happened. You were a good teacher, a good employee, someone with a "get things done" mentality, and others recognized that. Now they want you to be responsible for teaching other adults to do what you do. The great thing is that now you have an opportunity to have a positive impact on a greater number of people, and thus a greater number of children. The hard part is that most master teachers do what they do naturally, and making that leap from teacher to supervisor can take some work. But you can do it!

How Do You Feel about Being a Supervisor?

It's no mistake that you picked up this book. People who read want to learn more, and you want to learn more about supervision. You might be a supervisor or be thinking about supervising; or maybe a colleague or even your supervisor is encouraging you to read this book.

How do you feel about being a supervisor? You may be in one of the following positions:

- Exploring the idea of leading adults given your success with children.
- Ready for greater leadership opportunities within your teaching position.
- Eager to become a supervisor.
- Excited and nervous about being a supervisor for the first time. (Even positive change can be hard.)
- Reluctant to become a supervisor. Others encourage you to lead, but you are afraid.
- Committed to remain a teacher. We need master teachers. You may not carry the title of supervisor, but you still lead through role modeling and helping others.
- Hesitant about dealing with difficult supervisory situations. It's fun to lead when others are following, but more challenging to guide adults to change and grow.
- Comfortable with your leadership skills, but in need of more ideas to encourage and connect to staff.

Be honest with yourself about how you feel as a supervisor. Supervising can be difficult and complex, and no two people will accomplish it the same way. Your feelings about your position may vary from day to day, but it's good to have a sense of how you approach your position. As you read this book, you may find your feelings toward supervising changing—and that's okay too!

What Do Supervisors Do?

What do supervisors do? In the very basic sense, supervisors help adults to succeed just as teachers help children to succeed. Here are some more ideas. Supervisors do the following:

- Value children and families
- Guide and coach staff
- Build relationships
- Encourage innovation
- Role-model excellence

Does that sound like you? I forgot to include plunging the toilet—that's part of the job too. Being a supervisor in early childhood education is a challenging job at times but a thoroughly rewarding one. You have the opportunity to positively affect the lives of many children by encouraging the adults who teach them. Are you ready for the challenge? You are!

MARIELLE HAD WORKED IN THE TODDLER ROOM *at the Child Development Academy for almost three years. As a teacher, Marielle was organized, great with families and their children, and worked well with other staff. Many of the teachers in the toddler room and Marielle were friends outside of work and enjoyed going out for dinner on Friday nights and chatting over the phone. In fact, it was the team of teachers in her room who encouraged Marielle to apply for the lead teacher position when the former lead moved. "You'll make a wonderful lead teacher," they told her.*

Marielle went through the interview process and got the job. At first all the other teachers were happy for her. Slowly, as Marielle began to address issues in the room, ask them to do things that were not getting done, and tell them about new center policy, the other staff members weren't as excited about her new position as lead teacher. The other teachers started having conversations without her, and when they went to dinner, Marielle felt uncomfortable because the conversation inevitably led to complaints about the academy administrators, of which she was now one. Some teachers even pressed her to tell them confidential information.

Marielle was eager as a new supervisor to help improve the quality of care and education in her room and program, but supervising her friends was hard.

You Can Do It!

Learn to:

- ❑ Accept your role as a supervisor.
- ❑ Use your skills in working with children as a basis for supervising adults.
- ❑ Feel comfortable when people treat you differently because you are a supervisor.
- ❑ Gain the respect of the people you supervise and your supervisor.
- ❑ Have an impact on more adults and children as a supervisor.

Stay Positive! Avoid:

- ❑ Dodging difficult situations and conflict.
- ❑ Wanting everyone to like you.
- ❑ Working for the approval of others.
- ❑ Thinking you're not making a difference because you're not working directly with children all the time.

winning ways

Make It Happen! Here's How

Admit You're the Supervisor

Whether you wanted the promotion to supervisor or were encouraged by others, it's your title now. Many of the people who work in early childhood education do so because of their nurturing and encouraging spirit, and they feel uncomfortable telling other adults what to do. That's especially true when it comes to dealing with conflict or enforcing consequences for other adults' inappropriate behavior, such as being late, not completing paperwork on time, or having a negative attitude. Sound familiar?

We like to guide and lead others as long as everyone is doing what we say. But think about it: children don't always do what we say, and it takes a lot of patience and innovation to get children moving in the right direction. We wouldn't let children hit one another because we don't want to deal with conflict, so why would we let staff hurt one another with gossip or poor attitudes just because we don't want to deal with conflict?

SELF-ASSESSMENT

How Am I Doing "Admitting That I Am the Supervisor"?

Coming to terms with your position as supervisor can sometimes be hard. Look at the questions below and evaluate how comfortable you are in your supervisory role. Taking some time to assess your level of confidence and to think about why you feel the way you do can be helpful in understanding your role as supervisor.

1 I feel confident in my role as a supervisor.

Always   Usually   Sometimes   Never

List areas in which you feel unsure or insecure:

_____   _____

_____   _____

_____   _____

being a supervisor

2   I realize that I was promoted to supervisor because I am a good teacher and reliable employee.

Always   Usually   Sometimes   Never

Some of my best skills and talents include:

_____   _____

_____   _____

_____   _____

3   I have confidence in the skills I use to work with children, and I apply many of these same concepts in my supervision of adults.

Always   Usually   Sometimes   Never

What are some of the skills you use with children that also apply to working with adults?

_____

_____

_____

_____

4   I realize that as a supervisor I will be treated differently by staff.

Always   Usually   Sometimes   Never

Are there ways that your staff treats you now as a supervisor that make you feel good in your role? List them below.

_____

_____

_____

_____

Are there ways that your staff treats you now as a supervisor that make you feel sad or left out? Write them down.

_____

_____

_____

_____

5 I work to gain the respect of staff, not their approval.

Always   Usually   Sometimes   Never

What are some of the ways that you know your staff respects or is beginning to respect you?

_____

_____

_____

_____

Being a Master Supervisor

If you're really a master teacher, then you can be a master supervisor by applying the same techniques and skills to adults as you did with children; just lose the sweetsy voice. Too bad adults aren't as cute as kids.

Being a supervisor doesn't mean you're unfair or harsh. It means assuming authority, helping people, and also holding them accountable for their actions. Being a good supervisor means helping adults to be the very best they can be. So admit you're the supervisor and do the very best job you can.

Use Your Skills with Children to Guide Adults

What does a master teacher do? How does she engage the children? A master teacher:

- Develops individual relationships with each child.
- Celebrates a child's current skills and gives him opportunities to enhance and develop new skills.
- Provides a routine and clear expectations for the child.
- Validates a child's feelings of accomplishment, anger, or frustration.
- Helps the child resolve conflict with others.
- Redirects the child to appropriate behavior.
- Gives the child opportunities to learn self-help skills.

being a supervisor

There are more things we do with children, but let's take the preceding list and see how it can be applied to adults. As a supervisor, you can use the skills you use with children to coach and guide adults. In fact, your experience in the classroom gives you an edge that other professionals don't have as they move up the ladder. You can guide adults by:

- Developing an individual relationship with each staff member.

- Assessing and recognizing a staff member's current skills and giving her opportunities to enhance and develop new skills.

- Providing a specific job description and clear expectations for the staff member.

- Listening to a staff member's feelings of accomplishment, anger, or frustration, but expecting a solution-oriented attitude and united front.

- Helping the staff member resolve conflict with others.

- Redirecting and coaching a staff member to be more successful.

- Delegating tasks to a staff member that give her more opportunities to be self-sufficient.

Isn't it amazing how so many of the goals we have for children are the same as those for adults? Of course, with adults we expect greater accountability and responsibility. So you see, you have the skills to get started as a supervisor; you just need to apply them.

Some Similarities in Guiding Children and Guiding Adults

	Guiding Children	Guiding Adults
Relationships	Develops individual relationships with each child	Develops individual relationships with each staff member
Skills	Celebrates current skills	Recognizes and builds on current skills
Expectations	Conveys simple, age-appropriate expectations	Provides job descriptions and clear expectations
Emotions	Validates children's emotions and helps them to express their emotions appropriately	Listens to staff members' feelings and encourages a solution-oriented attitude
Conflict	Helps children learn to resolve conflict	Guides staff members to resolve conflict on their own and helps when necessary
Behavior	Redirects children to appropriate behavior	Coaches staff members to meet job expectations
Self-Sufficiency	Gives children opportunities to learn self-help skills	Delegates to help staff members become more self-sufficient

being a supervisor

Expect People to Treat You Differently

When you're a teacher, you're one of the teaching team. You work together, laugh together, and occasionally complain about the supervisors together. Although complaints should always go to the person with whom you have an issue, people who have common jobs usually develop common bonds. That common bond can create an unintentional separation between teachers and supervisors. Even when supervisors do everything they can to make staff feel respected and well treated, there will still be a division by virtue of the difference in titles, hierarchy, compensation, communication, meetings, and such.

As a supervisor you may still work in the classroom alongside other teachers doing many of the things they do, but you are still the supervisor, and because of that you hold a special role and are seen as different by the staff you supervise. Even those who were or are your friends may treat you differently than they used to. That's okay. You do have a new role now and you will be different. You may not be able to share all the information you once did because of confidentiality issues. You may be out of the room more often because of meetings and paperwork. You may not get invited to after-work social activities, because people may feel they can't talk freely around you.

Yes, you're the same person, but in your job, you really are different. You have different responsibilities and priorities, and often a different level of commitment to work.

Work for Respect, Not Approval

In a way, we really do want people to treat us differently. As supervisors, we want them to follow our lead, consider our suggestions, and complete our requests. Yet we often feel bad when everyone "doesn't like us" or "isn't our friend." At work we can certainly be friendly, but we can't expect everyone to be our friends, nor will we feel like being friends with everyone.

What should we expect as a supervisor? We should expect others to respect us but not necessarily to like us or even agree with us all the time. We should also expect others to feel comfortable questioning our decisions yet present a united front to families and children. And we should expect others to know that we will consistently communicate openly and honestly even when that means conveying difficult messages.

How to Gain Respect as a Supervisor

How do supervisors gain respect? Respect usually comes in two ways. Many staff members will give you respect simply because of your title and the authority that has been given to you. You will hold the respect of those people until you consistently through your performance give them reason not to respect you. For example, you may say that everyone has to be on time, yet you do not have consequences for those who are late or, even worse, are always late yourself. Consistent marginal performance on the part of you as the supervisor will result in lack of respect from your employees.

The second way that you receive respect as a supervisor is by earning it. For most teachers who are promoted through the ranks, and may still even work in the same classroom where you were a teacher, you will mostly likely have to earn the respect of the people you supervise. You were once working alongside other educators, and now you have to tell them what to do. There may be a feeling of "Why do we have to listen to her?" and that can be especially true if others whom you now supervise applied for the same job.

So how do you gain respect? Supervisors gain respect through consistent, demonstrated competence. In other words, you do a good job. And doing a good job means that you treat others with respect. Will you make mistakes as a supervisor? Oh yes. We all make mistakes. In those cases you should apologize and move on. If you find yourself repeatedly making the same mistakes, then you will need guidance from your own supervisor to succeed.

being a supervisor

Accepting your role as supervisor can be challenging. Admitting that you're the supervisor means knowing that your role has changed within your program. And for some supervisors, it may mean consistently performing well to earn others' respect for your new role. Either way, owning your position and being a courageous leader take time and dedication, but you can do it!

If you're committed to young children, then you'll care about the success of the adults on your team too. Read the next chapter to learn more about guiding adults to succeed just as you did for each child you cared for and educated.

OPTIMIZE YOUR KNOWLEDGE

1   Do you currently hold a **supervisory role**, or are you hoping to have one? What do you like about supervising others, or why do you want to be a supervisor?

_____

_____

_____

_____

2   Do you agree that supervising adults is **similar** to teaching children? Why or why not?

_____

_____

_____

_____

winning ways

3 Describe a supervisor you've had whom you **respected.** What did he or she do that earned your confidence?

_____

_____

_____

_____

being a supervisor

2

Help Adults Succeed

I help adults succeed by making my expectations clear and reasonable

- Always
- Usually
- Sometimes
- Never

AMIRA WAS A STAR PERFORMER *from the first day she started substituting at the Rainbow Child Care and Learning Center. She took a full-time position a few weeks after she started subbing and practically lived at the center. Amira organized shelves, rearranged the environment, created new lesson plans, and chatted confidently with family members.*

After only a few months, Amira became a supervisor for the preschool. She had a list of new curriculum ideas and field trips that thrilled the director and families, but the other teachers whom Amira supervised weren't happy.

Amira had few commitments at home, so she spent a great deal of time at the center and was disappointed and judgmental when others didn't want to stay late or come in on the weekends to work. She really pushed the teachers to try new things and expressed her disappointment with them when they didn't catch on as fast as she did. Some of the teachers said things such as, "We have a life out of the center too," and "I don't understand what she wants." The teachers in Amira's preschool classes were failing even though she was working so hard.

You Can Do It!

Learn to:

- ❑ Realize that adults, like children, innately want to succeed.
- ❑ Question whether your expectations are realistic and your communication is effective.
- ❑ Understand that what you say is not always what people hear.
- ❑ Communicate your expectations in a clear, specific manner.
- ❑ Eliminate doubt by asking people if they understand what they are supposed to do.

Stay Positive! Avoid:

- ❑ Assuming people know what to do and how to do it.
- ❑ Thinking that people will do things the same way you do. Chances are there's more than one right way to do something.
- ❑ Getting frustrated when adults don't "get it" the first time.
- ❑ Expecting people to embrace and be excited about change. Even good change is hard.

Make It Happen! Here's How

Get People to Do Their Jobs

All right, you've read chapter 1. You admit that you're the supervisor, and you're excited about your new role. Probably all you can think about are the new things you want to do in your program. You're full of ideas and energy, a strong work ethic, and lots of enthusiasm. So are you wondering why the people you supervise aren't as excited as you? Do you wonder why they may not be completing the work you ask them to do? One of the greatest challenges for a supervisor is realizing that some of your employees don't always share your commitment. Sometimes other adults do the things you've asked them, and sometimes they don't. Even if they do follow through, often they just don't do the work the way you would have wanted.

So how do you get the people whom you supervise to do the job you want them to do? Let's think back to working with children. If a child isn't functioning well in your program, perhaps having separation problems or misbehaving, you don't immediately say, "What's wrong with that child?" No, you look at yourself first; you look at your role as a teacher. *Did I set up the room appropriately? Are my expectations realistic? Have I given the child enough attention and support?* It's the same when working with adults.

You Help Children to Learn

Let's think about the child who's challenging. As early childhood professionals, we would never say, "I don't think that child's ever going to crawl, so don't worry about taking that one out of the bouncy seat." We would never work with a preschooler and say, "I don't think that child will ever learn to read. He doesn't need books." Never. As teachers, we would never give up on children. We love children, and we would do anything we could to help them be successful. If we have a child who doesn't want to participate in an art project but who likes cars, we do crazy things, such as saying, "Let's roll cars through paint."

For children, we spend a great deal of energy and creativity to develop an individual care and education plan. We create an environment and experiences that fit the child and investigate and use other resources so every child can succeed. Our efforts are endless. But when it comes to the adults, do we think the same way? Usually not. Usually we expect adults to know what to do when we hire them, and after some limited hours of orientation, those adults are on their own to succeed. When those same adults fail, then we give them our time, energy, and resources. Let's help adults, just as we help children, before adults fail. That's our job as supervisors.

Help Adults to Succeed; Don't Wait until They Fail

There aren't many people who wake up in the morning and say, "Today I am going to really mess up at work. First, I'll be late, then not watch the children, and after that forget to turn in my paperwork." Absolutely not! Adults, like children, don't want to fail. Most of your employees work hard to seek the approval and affirmation of others, the acceptance of a group, and the feeling of a job done well. Unfortunately, there are adults who may feel like failures or even losers because of their past experiences and the way others have treated them.

Your greatest role as a supervisor is to help adults be successful, to coach them, to teach them, to be a role model for them, just like you would do for any child. If you're a master teacher, you can be a master supervisor. But adults are often more difficult to teach because adults don't like change. We like the comfort of routine and consistency.

Change is hard for everyone. Think about your morning routine. If you drink coffee in the morning, how hard would it be to do without it? Think about going to the movies. Do you usually sit in the same spot, in the back of the theater, in the middle, on the aisle? We adults, like children, thrive on routine, and getting us to try new things—or even unlearn something we've been doing a long time—can be hard.

Have Realistic Expectations of Adults

As supervisors, we have to realize that we cannot control those around us. We can try to motivate others to perform, and we can control our response to others when they don't. Here's the situation. You are good at your job. You get things done. You have moved from teacher to supervisor. As a supervisor, your to-do list for the day may look something like this: hire two teachers, rewrite the parent manual, and paint the school—all by yourself. You know you have lists like this! And most of you actually get a lot of it accomplished. You are very focused and very task oriented.

But no matter how good you are, you must depend on the performance of others for your program to function well. There is no way you could actually run your center alone, no matter how much coffee you've had. Every single person on your team and in your center is important. That's why you have to build on the success of every adult. And here's the deal with most supervisors: we may be overachievers, and we may have unrealistic expectations of others.

Practice DAP for Adults

As supervisors, we need to remember that some of the people who are working for us are not performing or aspiring to perform at our level. That's okay. Our expectations as supervisors should be that each employee does her job at an acceptable level of competence, according to what we have asked. Are you expecting your staff to be exactly like you? If you are, then your expectations are unrealistic. Let's look at the to-do list of one of your employees: get up, go to work, be on time, and text a friend. Now, is this to-do list wrong? No. It's just not your to-do list. So part of helping adults to succeed is setting clear and appropriate expectations. Think about this. You know what DAP is, right? Developmentally appropriate practice. Do you use DAP for adults? Or do you want people to be just like you, on your skill level, with the same experience?

being a supervisor

Or do you see the strengths and successes of everyone you supervise and help them become better? Do you accept your employees where they are and guide them to learn and grow? You should.

How to Help Adults Succeed

- Appreciate the skills, talents, experience, and ambition of those you supervise.
- Build on the skills and talents of each employee.
- Never assume your employees know what you want them to do.
- Make your expectations simple and specific.
- Communicate your expectations in a variety of ways—verbal meeting, written statement.
- Clarify expectations by asking the employee to tell you what he believes you expect.
- Address safety issues when communicating expectations.
- Concentrate on one job goal at a time if an employee has several job expectations that are being completed.

Communicate Clear Expectations

- During the interview
- At the point of hire
- During orientation
- In job descriptions
- On center charts
- During one-on-one meetings
- During staff meetings
- At performance appraisals
- As an issue arises but not around the children

Overcome Barriers to Success

Sometimes supervisors get frustrated when employees don't perform what seem to us to be simple tasks. *Shouldn't they just know that? Shouldn't they just do that?* Not unless we have told them. But what if you have communicated clear, simple expectations to an employee and the job is still not getting done? Ask the staff member why she is not completing the job. She may tell you reasons or even excuses for not doing her job. These are called barriers. Often there are barriers that the employee has or perceives to have that keep her from being successful.

Even though an employee may know and understand what she is supposed to do, the employee may feel she can't perform her role because of barriers. It may sound like this. Supervisor: "Please make sure you take out the trash after lunch." The employee: "We don't have enough staff to leave the room," or "I don't have enough time before my break." Some of the barriers that employees acknowledge are legitimate, others may be incorrect perceptions, and others may just be excuses. Be careful to explore the situation before you make assumptions about the type of barrier an employee is dealing with. Don't assume that she is making an excuse for not doing her job until you explore the situation.

BARRIERS CAN BE:

- Time constraints
- Lack of coverage
- Limited materials
- Lack of experience
- Need for additional skills and training
- Level of confidence
- Fear of failure
- Lack of motivation

Your job as a supervisor is to actively listen to the barriers the employee identifies and help her eliminate or overcome those barriers. Some people are barrier spotters, but you have to be a barrier jumper. *How am I going to help this person get over this barrier?*

being a supervisor

Ideas to Eliminate Barriers

- Give employees choices.

- Solve the barrier issue as a team.

- Provide advice based on experience.

- Have the person attend a workshop.

- Role-model how to overcome the barrier.

- Provide encouragement.

- Acknowledge a job well done.

- Offer your time as a supervisor.

- Create a culture that allows employees to question authority.

Tips for Helping Adults Succeed

Just as you work with each child, help every adult where he or she is to become a better early childhood professional. That's really all you have to do. Change and growth in adults doesn't happen overnight. Realize that some employees will never attain your level of expertise, nor will they all want to become supervisors.

- **Offer choices.** Offer employees choices in how they carry out or perform job expectations. *We need a bulletin board for Week of the Young Child. What would you like to do?* Or perhaps, *Teachers are bunching up in a group and chatting on the playground when they should be interacting with the children. How can we make sure all the children are supervised outside?*

- **Give individual attention.** Give one-on-one attention to the employee through weekly meetings, working alongside the person in the classroom, taking the employee out to lunch, or talking on the phone about how the day went. *It was really fun to watch you interacting with your class this afternoon. I'm curious about your thoughts— how do you think it went today?*

- **Listen to the employee.** Listen carefully and respond to the employee's real and perceived barriers. *So what I understand from you is that you can't use the water table more often because the children get wet and don't have a change of clothes. Let's send out a note to parents to bring in more clothes.*

- **Be patient.** Recognize the importance of being patient and helpful while adults are learning. *I understand that it takes some time to get a new routine working well. You're not the only one having difficulty— we'll work it out eventually.*

- **Offer staff assistance.** Encourage staff to seek help from each other. *Dana, in Toddler Room 2, has a lot of good ideas for helping with transition. I can arrange for you to spend some time in her room.*

- **Know that change is hard.** Understand the intensity of feelings regarding change. *I realize that having family-style meals with children is messy and much harder than the adults serving. Why don't you just start with having family-style snack?*

- **Give help.** Intervene and help the employee before he is too frustrated or overwhelmed. *Let me help you get the children dressed to go outside.*

- **Let the employee vent.** Provide a culture that allows for venting, listen to the employee, repeat to see if you understand her feelings, and then help her deal with the issue. *It sounds like that parent could have spoken to you more politely. I'm sorry. I'll speak with her, but in the meantime we need to think of a way to make sure all of her child's things are ready to go at the end of the day. How can we do that?*

being a supervisor

SELF-ASSESSMENT

How Am I Doing "Helping Adults Succeed"?

Take a look at each of the statements below and assess your ability to help adults succeed. As you think about your supervising role, consider the feedback, intentional or unintentional, that employees have given you, and the ways that information can help you become a better supervisor.

1 I realize that teaching adults is my job as a supervisor.

Always   Usually   Sometimes   Never

List some things that you were surprised your employees didn't know.

_____   _____

_____   _____

2 I know that most adults want to succeed.

Always   Usually   Sometimes   Never

Write some ways you can help an employee be successful.

_____   _____

_____   _____

3 I understand that others may have barriers that prevent them from doing their jobs.

Always   Usually   Sometimes   Never

What are some of the barriers that employees have stated?

_____

_____

_____

_____

4 I help my employees overcome barriers.

Always   Usually   Sometimes   Never

List some of the ways you have helped your employees eliminate barriers to performing job expectations.

_____

_____

_____

_____

Sometimes it's difficult to know exactly how to help an employee succeed. In those situations, slow down and carefully think about the areas in which the employee is successful. Use those successful skills and talents to apply to other job responsibilities. By examining your own expectations and perceptions as well as what your employees are doing well and might be thinking, you can learn how better to coach others toward success. Use the following form to walk yourself through a coaching process by making sure each step is thoughtfully answered and applied. A good guideline keeps even the most successful supervisors on track. The form can be photocopied or downloaded from the *Being a Supervisor* page at www.redleafpress.org and distributed to your staff.

being a supervisor

Form 1   Building on Success: Coaching

1   What do you actually observe the employee doing? Is the behavior really what you think it is, or are you irritated, generalizing, or judgmental? Document what you see.

_____

_____

_____

_____

2   What are your expectations for the employee? Have you made your expectations specific? Write down your expectations.

_____

_____

_____

_____

3   How can you coach the employee to be successful? Are there barriers that the employee has or perceives that keeps him from being successful? What are those barriers?

_____

_____

_____

_____

4   Can you think of solutions to eliminating those barriers?

_____

_____

_____

_____

5   What resources can you think of to give the employee to help her be successful? How will you support her? What will you do?

_____

_____

_____

_____

It's easy to become frustrated with adults when they don't do things exactly the way you would do them. Helping adults succeed requires the same patience and commitment that you used as an early childhood educator working with children. Great supervisors not only communicate clear expectations, but they also want to know what the employees who work at the program are thinking; they want feedback, the good and the not-so-good. Successful supervisors also know that people will make mistakes as they learn and grow and simply while performing the everyday routines of their jobs. Expect some mistakes to happen along the way. I bet you've made some mistakes. I sure have. Check out chapter 3.

OPTIMIZE YOUR KNOWLEDGE

1   What are some **unspoken expectations** you have for your employees, whether they are being met or not? How can you make those expectations clear?

_____

_____

_____

_____

2   Interview two other supervisors about **how they help their team succeed**. What kinds of unmet expectations are frustrating to them? How do they deal with failure? Write some of their answers and ideas here.

_____

_____

_____

_____

3   Take some time to think about the adults you supervise. What are some of their **strengths and skills**? Are there certain skills they have that you could utilize more fully? If you are not currently a supervisor, list a couple of traits of a former supervisor that she fully utilized.

_____

_____

_____

_____

being a supervisor

3

Create a Culture That Encourages Input and Allows for Mistakes

I encourage input from my team and understand that mistakes happen.

- ○ Always

- ○ Usually

- ○ Sometimes

- ○ Never

AS A SUPERVISOR, SHAI CONCENTRATED *mostly on the front end of her job. She focused on paperwork, attended meetings, and did a lot of extra projects that pleased her own supervisor, the director.*

Shai gave her employees little attention unless they did something wrong. Then she was quick to point out the problem and tell employees what she wanted them to do to fix the problem. The staff could tell that she was angry even if the simplest thing went wrong. "She just cares what the director thinks about her," noted one teacher.

Shai rarely walked through the classrooms and knew little about the families and children. Since no one told her otherwise, Shai thought things were going well in her rooms and all the staff was satisfied. She was surprised to learn that the teachers finally went to the director with their concerns and ideas. The director asked the staff to speak directly to Shai. The staff told Shai, "You only talk to us when you are upset. We never get a chance to talk to you about our ideas and thoughts about the program."

You Can Do It!

Learn to:

- ❑ Encourage staff to tell you what they are thinking.
- ❑ Motivate others to give their best.
- ❑ Make it easy for employees to provide input.
- ❑ Ask people what they think.
- ❑ Realize that making mistakes is part of learning, even for adults.

Stay Positive! Avoid:

- ❑ Thinking you know everything and always have the best ideas.
- ❑ Soliciting employees' ideas and not using them or responding.
- ❑ Not really listening when someone has input.
- ❑ Not giving credit and recognition for the ideas and suggestions of others.

Make It Happen! Here's How

Create a Culture That Encourages Input and Allows for Mistakes

As a supervisor, your greatest strength is your staff. When each person you supervise is actively engaged in performing his or her current responsibilities and looking for ways to make things more efficient and better for children and families, you're doing your job: you're motivating and teaching adults. Your employees are full of ideas, suggestions, and opinions, many positive and some unfavorable. It's easy for supervisors to alienate themselves unintentionally from their staff by going about their "supervisor" responsibilities and not really knowing what their employees are doing or thinking. Many employees express, "My supervisor only notices me when I mess up." It's also comfortable for supervisors to assume that "what we don't know won't hurt us." Having information and acting on that information is key to our success. For you to do the best for your program and for the children, you need to know what your employees are thinking. What are they thinking about the environment, the curriculum, school policies, the families they serve, the children; and especially, what are they thinking about you?

being a supervisor

Gain the Perspective of Others

Teachers and other staff have a unique perspective of being hands-on in the room, and from their position we can learn a lot about how to provide better care and education for the children. And that's what it's all about, isn't it? How can we make things better for the children and families we serve?

Anyone old enough to remember rotary phones? How about party lines? And I'm not talking about 1-800 infomercials on late-night television. No, I'm talking about the old-fashioned phone system where two or three families shared the same phone line. You might pick up the phone in your home and hear your neighbor having a conversation on his phone. You had to wait until he was through in order to use the phone.

Well, imagine that no one ever thought about improving the quality of phone service. How did we get from rotary phones to cellular phones? Input, ideas, suggestions. Imagine that technology in medicine never advanced. What if surgeons still used ether to sedate people during operations? Ouch!

So if innovations and ideas are good, why are we so resistant to getting ideas and input from those who work for us? Do we think our program is good enough? Do we think we have all the answers and know how to do things just the right way? Our employees are sources of input and innovation. All we have to do is ask them what they think and act on it! If you are afraid to ask because you don't know what you will hear, then you really need to know.

Create an Environment Where People Feel Safe to Share Their Thoughts

So how are you going to know what people are thinking? There are lots of ways to create a culture that encourages input, but keep in mind that people will talk to you and really tell you how they feel if you create a safe environment for them to speak. How do you create a safe environment? A safe environment is one in which:

- No question or suggestion is ever dismissed as "dumb."
- People are not judged for what they say.
- Everyone's opinion is respected.
- Others really listen to what people are saying.
- Many of the ideas and suggestions are considered and used.
- Praise and recognition are given, not just for favorable outcomes, but when people try new ideas and contribute to discussions or brainstorming sessions.

Remember the discussion in chapter 2 about DAP (developmentally appropriate practice) for adults? Just like children, some adults will talk to us freely when we ask them, some will tell us what's on their minds even if we don't ask them, but many won't respond. You might say, "How are things going in your room?" and the employee responds, "Fine," when you know she is upset about her coworker. We have to give adults a variety of ways to communicate safely with us, sometimes directly, sometimes in writing, sometimes by surveys, and even through another employee if someone is not bold enough to speak directly to us.

Responding to Input Doesn't Necessarily Mean Implementing It

We want to collect as much information about our program from as many sources as possible, create a culture that is safe for people to share information, and help each individual gain more confidence in sharing her ideas in a professional and productive manner. Are we going to be able to use every idea and put each suggestion into action? No. Even some good ideas aren't going to be implemented because of lack of personnel, resources, or time. There will also be input that is not valid. *All the parents are complainers.* That's probably not true, but we can listen to the employee and help him focus on the parent who is upset, figure out why, and take steps to help the parent feel more satisfied. *We should have a 1:2 ratio in the infant room.* That would improve quality. We know small groups are better for children, but financially that ratio is not feasible.

Creating a culture that encourages input doesn't mean we listen to employees who themselves are chronic complainers (that's a performance issue that needs to be formally addressed) or put into action every good idea that comes along. Creating a culture that encourages input means we value what others think, really listen to their thoughts, and know that the quality of our program is based on the collaborative effort of every employee on our team.

being a supervisor

Ways to Learn What Employees Are Thinking

1 Ask people what they think.

Ask people verbally for their input. Some people will speak comfortably and others will not say a word. Try asking people in various ways, such as one-on-one, in small meetings of a few people, or in large groups.

How do you think we should handle the transition as children move up to the next room?

I noticed you were quiet when that parent came in the classroom. Did she upset you?

2 Talk to people over the phone.

Many people will speak to you and feel less embarrassed and anxious if they speak over the phone. The telephone provides a safe exchange where people do not have to look each other in the eye. Some staff will also feel more comfortable not being in your office or in the center where they could be overheard. Remember to be sensitive to employees' personal time and priorities.

Things seem a bit stressed in your classroom. When we met as a group, you didn't have much to say, but I had the feeling there were things you wanted to discuss. Would you like to talk sometime over the phone after work?

3 Give people short, easy surveys to complete.

You can do a two-minute survey in which you ask people to tell you something that went well last week and then tell you something they'd like to do differently. By asking others what they would do differently, you're not insinuating that things went wrong or that there is a problem. You're just asking how they would do things.

Look at the questions that follow and notice that it's important to ask for the positive information first. We want to hear what is going well first so we can make sure to keep doing that. *What's one thing that worked well last week? Something good that happened? Now, what's one thing that you would have done differently?*

There are lots of ways of asking for input from your staff. One way is a simple "Let's Hear from You" survey that gets you and your employees thinking about the wonderful and the frustrating parts of the job, and how you as a supervisor can respond to that. Check out the form on the following page for an example. It can be photocopied or downloaded from the *Being a Supervisor* page at www.redleafpress.org and distributed to your staff.

Form 2   Let's Hear from You   Name (Optional):_____

1   I first knew I would like it here when

_____

_____

2   The nicest thing a parent ever said to me was

_____

_____

3   I want to pull my hair out when

_____

_____

4   The most endearing moment I've ever experienced at the school was

_____

_____

5   My biggest struggle here has been

_____

_____

6   It's so helpful when

_____

_____

7   After reading the handbook, the thing(s) that stood out most in my mind was

_____

_____

8   If I could change one thing here, I'd change

_____

_____

9   If I could share something with someone else on her first day of work, I would tell her

_____

_____

10   I feel like I am wasting my time when

_____

_____

11   When I think about my classroom, the first thing that comes to mind is

_____

_____

12   I'm proud to work here because

_____

_____

being a supervisor

4 Have meetings.

Meet with staff teams as a whole group (read more about when and how to have meetings in chapter 5). Some people are more willing to talk in a meeting than they are one-on-one with you. They often feel safer with a group of people. Think about children again. A parent tells us that his child never eats green beans at home, yet at the center, the child eats green beans as he sees the others eating.

A staff member in a meeting might think, "The other teacher is speaking up and the supervisor is listening, so I think I'll tell the supervisor what I'm thinking." There's safety in numbers!

5 Be available.

Just being available is another way you can find out what people are thinking. People are more likely to tell you what's on their minds if you're physically present.

Walk through the classrooms, have lunch with the teachers, keep your office door open when you don't mind being interrupted, and vary your shift so that you see the beginning and end of the day.

6 Have a staff representative system.

As I mentioned earlier, some people have difficulty speaking up for themselves. Should they learn to develop more confidence? Sure, but in the meantime, we can give them a way to voice their opinions and also develop a professional system that solicits people's ideas and suggestions. This system is especially beneficial if you have a larger center where it is impossible to physically connect with all your employees. People will talk whether we have a culture that allows it or not. Wouldn't you rather have employees bringing you their concerns than only chatting behind your back in the parking lot?

Here's how a staff rep system works. A staff member represents a group of other employees, such as all the toddler teachers or all the teachers in one classroom. The representatives from the various groups ask each individual in their group for input and then share it with the supervisor of that group. One way to help staff representatives structure their feedback is to use the Staff Representative Form on the next page. It can be photocopied or downloaded from the *Being a Supervisor* page at www.redleafpress.org and distributed to your staff.

winning ways

Form 3 Staff Representative Form

Group:

Staff Representative's Name:

Date:

Our Appreciations, Thank-Yous, and "Good Things" Happening in the Program

_____

_____

_____

_____

_____

_____

Our Ideas, Questions, and Concerns

_____

_____

_____

_____

_____

_____

Ways to Implement Our Ideas and Deal with Our Concerns

_____

_____

_____

_____

_____

_____

being a supervisor

7 Use a suggestion box.

Using a suggestion box might seem somewhat archaic, and it is if the box is hidden under papers and full of dust.

A real suggestion box can work this way:

- Display the suggestion box in a prominent, convenient place with paper and pens.

- Take the suggestions you receive each week and retype them.

- Respond to the suggestion or issue. If the person leaves her name, address her directly.

- Remember, a response doesn't always mean implementing an idea or making a change. Sometimes it's just clarifying communication and helping people to understand what is happening or what is supposed to happen.

- Hang the retyped suggestions and a short response to each one by the box so that everyone can benefit from the information.

- Show people that the box does not lead to oblivion and that someone does read the suggestions.

Be Open to New Ideas

All right, we know what people are thinking, but are we really open to their input? Can we honestly say, "I realize that my way is not the only way, and I am open to new ideas, suggestions, and comments, even unfavorable ones?" Once again, employees are going to talk regardless of whether you know about what they say or not. They're going to talk on the playground, they're going to talk in the parking lot, and they're going to call each other at night. And they usually talk because of a lack of communication, an absence of information, and a culture that doesn't encourage input.

We might be great at giving out surveys and having meetings, but do we have an open mind for the input of others? Do we really listen to our employees and feel that they have something valuable to contribute? Are you really listening?

How to Be a Good Listener

____ I give employees my full attention. I do not allow others to interrupt by telephone or physical presence.

____ I really listen. I do not form an opinion or start to respond until the person is finished talking.

____ I value what employees have to say even though I may not agree with them.

____ I show interest by asking questions.

____ I demonstrate understanding by repeating what the person says.

____ I try not to get defensive or to rationalize when the employee speaks.

____ I am conscious of my body language and tone of voice, trying not to convey annoyance or frustration.

____ I listen knowing that the people I work with have ideas and suggestions that will help me grow and learn.

____ I follow up with the employee about our conversation and what will happen next.

____ I am quick to give the employee credit and recognition for new ideas and input.

____ I thank the employee for coming to me and encourage him to talk with me as he needs.

Allow for Some Mistakes

Obviously in early childhood education, where we are serving children, we can't allow for mistakes or failures that compromise a child's safety. We need to have many systems and checks in place to ensure coverage is met, environments are safe, evacuation plans are complete, and much more. These policies and systems require frequent updating and improving. And that's where a culture that encourages input comes into play. We need to continually ask ourselves and our staff, "How can we make things better?"

When employees are putting their input to action, learning new skills, and trying new things, some mistakes will happen. Failure is a part of learning. Look at children. Toddlers don't take their first steps without a few tumbles, and preschoolers don't learn to write their names without learning to scribble.

being a supervisor

Can we give adults a chance to grow and learn and make mistakes? Perhaps a learning center could be better positioned or a memo could have been more precise? We need to give staff a chance to try new things, take risks, and make mistakes. We encourage input when we implement these guidelines:

- **Don't punish simple, nonrepetitive mistakes.** *The memo you wrote to the parents about bringing in extra clothes was well written, but it had a few typos. Next time let me or someone else read your memo before you send it out.*

- **Do reward admission of mistakes.** *Thank you for telling me that you forgot to stock the supplies. Let's make a checklist that we can hang in the class so you and others don't forget.*

- **Admit our own mistakes.** *I shouldn't have corrected you in front of the other teacher. I'm sorry. Next time we'll have a private conversation.*

Give Employees an Opportunity to Vent

We should expect employees to be professional and respectful at all times, but we shouldn't expect them not to have intense emotional feelings, sometimes called griping and complaining. As supervisors, we want people to tell us what is on their minds, especially if they are upset. Having an appropriate emotional reaction, like crying, often shows an employee's passion for her job.

We allow children to vent. Take a look. Suppose a child gets angry because someone knocks down his block tower and he hits the other child. We all know that the hitting part is not okay, but it is very appropriate for the child to be angry. We might say, "I know you're angry because he knocked down your blocks, but you can't hit him. Use your words and tell him no." Then we would probably redirect the child to build his tower again or even work cooperatively with the other child.

Shouldn't we allow adults to vent a little too? No, adults can't hit each other or be emotional all the time, but we do need to take time to help redirect their emotions and help solve the issue that is challenging them.

SELF-ASSESSMENT

How Am I Doing "Creating a Culture That Encourages Input and Allows for Mistakes"?

Do you allow your staff members to make mistakes and offer input? Let's see how well with the assessment below. It can be difficult for employees to give suggestions and difficult for supervisors to hear them. Take the following self-assessment to see how you're doing at creating a culture of openness and responsibility, and brainstorm some ways you could do even better.

1   I realize that each one of my employees has good ideas and suggestions.

Always   Usually   Sometimes   Never

List some of the ways you encourage employees to contribute their ideas.

_____   _____

_____   _____

_____   _____

2   I know that some adults won't feel comfortable voicing their input.

Always   Usually   Sometimes   Never

Think of a specific employee from whom you rarely hear and list some of the ways you might develop a better relationship with him and learn what he is thinking.

_____   _____

_____   _____

_____   _____

being a supervisor

3   I know what my staff is thinking, even the unfavorable things.

Always   Usually   Sometimes   Never

Think about an unfavorable response you received recently and write down how you learned the information and what you did to correct the issue.

_____

_____

_____

_____

4   I am a good listener.

Always   Usually   Sometimes   Never

List some of the ways you are working to become a better listener and some of the ways in which you listen well.

_____

_____

_____

_____

Hey, let's admit it: sometimes we don't really want to know what our employees think unless it's all good; and that's never the case, so remember, sometimes asking for feedback can be as difficult as giving it. As a supervisor, you can serve your employees better by being open to new ideas and understanding of mistakes and mishaps. It may initially hurt a bit to know that we are not perfect and things need to improve, but all great supervisors want a great program. After all, even children need our patience when they mess up, and as teachers, we are always learning how to guide children better. Getting feedback from your team can help you guide adults better as well. Another important part of leadership is entrusting leadership to others. That's what chapter 4 is all about. It's called delegation. Are you ready?

OPTIMIZE YOUR KNOWLEDGE

1 What makes someone an **approachable** supervisor? What are qualities that you've valued in leaders in the past?

_____

_____

_____

_____

2 List a few ways you might ask for **feedback** from employees. Consider what would make you more or less likely to give honest feedback, and consider others who are completely different from you.

_____

_____

_____

_____

3 How do you usually **respond** when adults need to "vent"? Are there ever times to allow or not allow the expression of feelings and perspective?

_____

_____

_____

_____

being a supervisor

4

Motivate Adults through Delegation

I motivate the adults on my team by delegating meaningful tasks.

- Always
- Usually
- Sometimes
- Never

SIMONE WAS AN EXTREMELY CAPABLE TEACHER. *As a supervisor, she used her organizational skills to create charts and lists of everything her employees were supposed to do. She arranged the room, wrote all the lessons plans, and conducted all the conferences with the parents. Simone even made or brought in lunch for her staff each month. All her employees had to do was follow her detailed plans.*

One of her staff members offered to help with the lesson plans, but Simone declined her offer and said she could do it herself. Simone thought to herself, "She'll never be able to do it as good as me."

Over time, Simone began to realize that she did most of the work and that the more she did, the less her staff did. "Why is my staff so unmotivated?" she wondered.

You Can Do It!

Learn to:

- ❑ Empower others to learn and grow through delegation.
- ❑ Utilize the skills and talents of each employee.
- ❑ Help people feel utilized, not used.
- ❑ Allow adults to use their own ideas and creativity to get the job done.

Stay Positive! Avoid:

- ❑ Making everyone "do it your way."
- ❑ Delegating only custodial or menial tasks that do not require creativity and ingenuity.
- ❑ Redoing an employee's work because you want it done your way.

Make It Happen! Here's How

Motivate Adults through Delegation. Don't Stand in the Way of Success

Can you let the process and results of a job be different from the way you would do it? Try to avoid the "do it my way" approach to supervision. Employees whose work is constantly criticized or redone because there is only one way to get things done eventually stop trying. And guess what? You're on your own to "do it your way." Everyone has skills and talents. Emphasize the skill or goal rather than the process or method. Allow freedom of expression. Don't stand in the way of teachers doing their job. Delegate a job and stand back. You'll be surprised and your employees will feel empowered, trusted, and proud! Build on success. There's more than one way to get things done.

Let Go of Control

Supervisors become supervisors because they are good at their jobs. Those of us in the early childhood education field moved up the ranks because we're really good with children. We're good at fingerpainting. We're good at making snacks with children. We're really good at teaching and caring for children, which doesn't necessarily translate into working well with adults.

being a supervisor

The administrators of your program saw the excellent performance you had in the classroom; they wanted you to help all the other teachers perform just like you. Unfortunately, no one else is like you. Just like children, teachers are all different.

As a new supervisor or even a seasoned one, you're likely to hold on tightly to the reins of control, feeling that if you tell everyone exactly what to do and how to do it, they will do it just like you. Voilà! But it doesn't work that way. Supervision is not about getting people to act like us; it's about getting them to act and perform the very best they can. For people to be motivated to do their best, they need the freedom to take on new responsibilities, use their creativity, and do things "their way."

SELF-ASSESSMENT

Don't Get in the Way of Success: Delegation

Can you let the process and results of a job be different from the way you would do it? Try to avoid the "do it my way" approach to supervision. There's more than one way to get things done. Use the questions below to help you think through your own approach to delegating or keeping control. Are you a control freak or even on the edge of becoming one?

1 Have you ever redone a job you delegated to another employee? If so, give an example.

_____

_____

2 Think of one employee. List three skills or talents she has.

1 _____

2 _____

3 _____

3 Describe a job you could delegate to that employee that would utilize those skills or talents.

_____

_____

4 Describe a job you like to be completed a certain way, and comment on what would happen if an employee did the job differently.

_____

_____

_____

_____

Maintain Accountability

Here's the even more difficult part: although we cannot get others to act like us, we are nevertheless accountable for how they act. That's tough. As a supervisor you are ultimately accountable for everything that happens in your program area, even if you delegate a task to someone else. _If I delegate a task and the person messes up, then I'm responsible for his mistakes._ So are you thinking, _Why would I delegate and risk failure when I know I can do it myself?_ You delegate because you can't do it all by yourself, at least not for long. Nor should you.

12 Reasons to Delegate

1 You can't accomplish the work by yourself.

2 The quality of work will be better when you allow and depend on the input and help of others. (Remember chapter 3?)

3 Delegating tasks will free you to concentrate on other priorities.

4 Employees feel motivated and appreciated by delegation that utilizes their skills.

5 You learn from others.

6 Your employees can often do a better job than you. (Your job is not to do all the work but to make sure it gets done and gets done well. Why not let the person who is best at the job do the job?)

7 Employees learn to be more confident.

8 You identify other potential leaders in your program.

9 Employees are challenged.

10 Staff members are usually more satisfied with their jobs when they have greater responsibility.

11 Delegation builds relationships as you monitor employees' progress and provide support for their tasks.

12 A sense of satisfaction prevails when employees complete their tasks.

being a supervisor

Why We Avoid Delegation

Even though we know delegation is essential to successful supervision, most of us don't do it well. Read the following statement aloud:

I don't try to do everything myself, and I rely on others.

There's a word for that statement. *Delegate*. Delegate means giving someone else a task for which you are ultimately responsible. Do you like to delegate? Do you prefer not to delegate? Why don't we delegate?

There are a lot of reasons why we don't like to delegate. *They won't do it like us. It takes too long to tell them.* Let's focus on taking too long for a second. You might think, "By the time I tell the employee what to do, I could have done it myself." Anyone guilty of that reason? By not taking the time to delegate, you deprive the employee of an opportunity to learn.

Imagine if you said this to a child: "Don't bother zipping your coat. I can do it much faster than you. It takes fifteen minutes for you to do the zipper thing, so just let me zip it up." What happens then? You end up with children who can't zip.

We don't want to end up with adults who aren't competent, who "can't zip." We deprive others of opportunities to learn when we don't delegate. You are still accountable regardless of what you delegate, but you need to start letting go of some of the tasks, releasing the control. Delegating motivates people and gives them a chance to learn. If delegation is implemented properly, it is the best way to run an organization. We have to delegate whether we like it or not.

Reasons Why We Avoid Delegating

- Supervisors are afraid to relinquish control.
- Supervisors are afraid to fail.
- Supervisors want things done exactly as they would do them.
- Supervisors are perfectionists.
- Supervisors are not willing to take risks.
- Supervisors are afraid someone else won't do a good job.
- Supervisors are afraid someone else might do a better job.
- Supervisors don't take the time to explain the task to another.
- Supervisors don't trust their employees.

Why Some Employees Find Delegation Difficult

Just as it can be difficult for supervisors to delegate, some employees can find delegation difficult too. We finally get enough courage to give up the control and delegate the task, and then the employee resists it. Now what? The number one reason people don't want to try new things is fear of failure. They're afraid. Another reason people are averse to delegation is because they know you want it done your way. In early childhood education, we realize that some tasks must be performed in a specific, accurate, unfaltering way: the dispensing of medication, the completion of certain forms, the disinfecting of toys, but whenever possible, empower employees to do things their way.

Utilize People; Don't Use Them

Another reason employees are resistant to the delegation of tasks is that they feel *used*, not *utilized*. Using someone means always delegating custodial or menial tasks that require little ingenuity or creativity, like telling people to vacuum or to restock the diapers. Utilizing someone is learning her skills and preferences and delegating tasks that match her strengths and drive. Now, the floors must be cleaned and the diapers stocked, but if that's all you ever ask someone to do, she won't have much of a chance to grow and learn. And of course, there are those people who are good at cleaning and organizing and like to do it. Thank goodness.

If supervisors never delegate tasks that motivate individual employees, we are just using them. If I never give you anything that makes you feel good, that lets you shine, that makes you feel like you've learned something, I just use you. When I give an employee a task that challenges her, creates a sense of personal satisfaction, and brings her recognition and praise, then I utilize her. Are you using employees or utilizing them?

Reasons Employees Resist Delegation

- Employees are afraid to fail. *He gets so mad if I mess up. I'd rather not even try.*

- Employees know the supervisor only wants it done "his way." *Maybe he should just do it. He usually redoes my work anyway.*

- Employees feel like the supervisor is taking advantage of them. *He does all the fun work and gives me all the nothing jobs.*

- Employees don't understand what they are supposed to do. *He just assumes I know what to do. He didn't give me any details or directions.*

being a supervisor

- Employees do not receive any feedback for their work. *He didn't say anything about the project he gave me. I'd rather hear something bad than nothing at all.*

- Employees are not recognized for their efforts. *He asks me to do all this work, and then he never thanks me. Sometimes he even takes credit for what I did.*

Understand What Motivates People

Employees are motivated when they have competent supervisors who help them succeed, and good delegation is part of that success. Employees want to be:

- Listened to
- Given attention
- Respected
- Challenged
- Given interesting work
- Given help and support as they work
- Able to see the results of their work
- Recognized and praised

Challenge Professional Growth

There's really nothing you can't delegate, or at least a part of it, from bulletin boards to budget development to staff coverage. Here are a few ideas of things to delegate. Add a couple of your own ideas of things that you can delegate to challenge an employee's professional growth and yours too. Giving up the control will help you become a better supervisor.

winning ways

Employees can:

Develop a special activity for the classroom or center

Handle coverage when a teacher is absent

Mentor a new coworker

Take potential parents on center tours

Design a classroom or center newsletter

Handle a petty cash account

Select and purchase items for the classroom

_____

_____

Delegation Tips

- Offer adults choices in what additional jobs they want to try.
  Would you like to organize our next preschool field trip or the Mother's Day Tea?

- Encourage adults and help them to overcome their fears to complete new tasks. *We'll work on the field trip together. Make a list of the places you'd like to take the children, and I'll help you set up the trip after we make a decision.*

- Provide experiences for adults that offer challenges yet allow them to experience success. *If you don't feel like you can do the whole newsletter, just write one article about what the children have been doing in your class.*

- Help adults recognize their skills and use them. *You did a terrific job on the display in your classroom that shows photographs of children building with blocks. I want you to do a similar display for the center lobby.*

being a supervisor

- Give the adult a simple explanation of the work you are delegating and have her demonstrate her understanding by providing you with a plan or telling you what she is going to do. *Please organize and label the manipulative shelf in your classroom by Friday. Show me an example of one of the labels before you get started on the whole shelf.*

- Use articles, forms, illustrations, discussions, and other examples to help clarify the job you are delegating. *Take a look at this photograph from the catalog. Please label the shelves similar to this. Do you notice how the pictures and words are easy to see?*

- Ask the adult who is more skilled and confident if she has a way that she would like to complete the task. *I would like for you to do a family information board for the center lobby. Think about some ideas and let me know by the end of the week what you plan on doing.*

- Give adults a chance to improve their skills by your delegating the task again. *Your parent-teacher conference went well. You really made the parent feel comfortable. Here are a few tips to make your next conference even better.*

- Pair two employees with similar skills and expertise. Camaraderie reduces tension and the fear of failure. *Since you both attended the state conference, I want you to work together to write one page of ideas you learned and share it at the next staff meeting.*

- Have a less experienced employee work with someone who is more seasoned. *This week work with Tonya on staff coverage, and next week you can take it on yourself. She'll still be there if you need any help or have questions.*

SELF-ASSESSMENT

How Am I Doing "Motivating Adults through Delegation"?

Supervisors often become supervisors because they are so capable themselves, but it requires a different skill set to hand over a project to someone else. Think about your own comfort level with delegating to adults. It might also help to remember a time when a supervisor offered, or witheld from you, a project you knew you were capable of. How did that affect your performance as an employee? With regard to delegation, evaluate your supervising honestly using the assessment below.

1 I empower others to grow and learn through delegation.

Always   Usually   Sometimes   Never

Do you have a hard time delegating certain tasks? List three things that you would like to delegate but have not because you feel afraid or unsure:

1 _____

2 _____

3 _____

Why is it difficult to delegate these tasks, and what could you do to at least delegate a small portion?

_____

_____

_____

2 I allow others to use their own skills and talents when I delegate.

Always   Usually   Sometimes   Never

Think of some of the tasks you can delegate. Which ones must be completed a certain way, and which ones can allow for creativity?

Tasks That Must Be Uniform

_____

_____

_____

Tasks That Allow for Creativity

_____

_____

_____

being a supervisor

3   I utilize people, not use them.

Always   Usually   Sometimes   Never

List some of your job responsibilities that you really like.

1 _____

2 _____

3 _____

List some of the job responsibilities that you don't like.

1 _____

2 _____

3 _____

Do you delegate the responsibilities you like and the ones you don't like fairly, or do you tend to give people the work you don't like?

_____

_____

_____

Review the lists of jobs you like and don't like. Determine which ones you could delegate. To whom could you delegate them? Often it's most difficult to give up, to delegate, the pieces of your job that you really enjoy.

_____

_____

_____

Can you think of an experience when you've been motivated to work hard and contribute to the team and your supervisor encouraged you and even praised you? It feels good, right? Supervisors who are able to delegate significant work to their employees can inspire the whole team toward a common goal. Your employees will trust you more, and you'll be sharing the workload with a capable team: everyone wins!

In chapter 5, I cover another way everyone wins, through consistent, honest communication.

winning ways

OPTIMIZE YOUR KNOWLEDGE

1   Describe in your own words what it means to **delegate**.

_____

_____

_____

_____

2   **Name three things** you delegate most often and three things you
are reluctant to delegate. How could you delegate at least one of the
things you are least likely to delegate?

1 _____

2 _____

3 _____

3   Explain the difference between **using and utilizing** employees.

_____

_____

_____

_____

being a supervisor

5

Communicate Consistently and Honestly

I communicate information and feedback consistently to my team.

- ○ Always

- ○ Usually

- ○ Sometimes

- ○ Never

SYDNEY WORKED AS A LEAD TEACHER *alongside the other teachers she supervised. Her preschool team functioned well. Sydney had created a working environment where the teachers felt comfortable trying new ideas to improve the program. Everyone participated in planning and carrying out fun and educational activities for the children.*

Sydney was surprised when one of the teachers on her team told her that another employee did not supervise the children well when Sydney wasn't there. "She just sits down while the children are playing. She doesn't interact with them, and sometimes it seems like she's not even watching them," the teacher complained to Sydney.

Although Sydney felt like she should say something to the employee in question, she never saw this behavior herself and didn't want to upset the employee by discussing it. "I'll just wait until I see the same thing," thought Sydney.

A few weeks later a child in the preschool room wandered into the hall when the teacher in question was supervising the children.

You Can Do It!

Learn to:

❑ Communicate consistently as much information as you can to your employees unless it is confidential.

❑ Determine what feedback is beneficial to helping a person succeed and learn.

❑ Give honest performance feedback even if it is difficult.

Stay Positive! Avoid:

❑ Letting marginal performance continue.

❑ Sugarcoating difficult messages.

❑ Withholding information or being secretive.

Make It Happen! Here's How

Use Honest Communication

Those of us in early childhood education are usually very nurturing people, sensitive to the feelings of others, and eager to resolve or avoid conflict if necessary. These are all great traits, especially since we are caring for and educating children. Sometimes, however, these nurturing traits and tendencies to avoid conflict keep us from communicating honestly with others.

Honest communication is not about hurting someone's feelings or acting superior or judging others. Honest communication is about accurately identifying, through observation or experience, a behavior or pattern of behaviors that indicates a need for change, then consistently communicating that observation to the person and being willing to help that individual improve. In other words, *It looks to me like you need help, and I want to help you.* It can be photocopied or downloaded from the *Being a Supervisor* page at www.redleafpress.org and distributed to your staff.

being a supervisor

winning ways

Why Is Honest Communication Important?

Honest communication is important because it is a tool that allows us to help others. Think about an infant in your care who doesn't appear to be developing gross-motor strength in his legs. The infant is not putting weight on his legs when you hold him and is not trying to pull up. Would you avoid telling the parents your concerns? Initially perhaps, until you confirm your observations. You might go back and document your observations over a period of time and consult with the director to see if she notices the same gross-motor concern about the child.

Observe, Document, and Consult

After careful observation, documentation, and consultation, you see the same lack of gross-motor development in the infant. Would you avoid telling the parents because they might initially deny your observation or get mad at you? No. You'd tell the parents because you know that telling could help the child. But what if your observations were wrong? In this case, all the better. The child's pediatrician examines the child, finds his gross-motor strength is developing a bit slower than what is typical but within an appropriate range, and we move on. You were concerned enough about the child to communicate honestly to the parents even if they didn't believe you, even if they got angry at you, and even if you were wrong. You communicated honestly because you wanted to help the child.

Help Someone, Even If It Is Difficult

Can you do the same for adults? Are you willing to tell them what you notice about their performance even if it's a difficult conversation to have? Or will you just let things go until the issue becomes a problem that you can no longer ignore? Honest communication means telling your employees about all the good things they are doing, but it also means telling them your concerns and giving them constructive feedback and support.

Tell Others When They Have "Broccoli in Their Teeth"

If someone had a concern about your performance, wouldn't you want to know? We want to know what people are saying about us, even if it's unfavorable. Did you ever go to a party where you were having a great time and chatting with everyone? Later you head to the bathroom, look at yourself in the mirror, and say, "What is that between my teeth?" You had something stuck in your teeth, like a piece of broccoli or lettuce, and no one told you. You've been walking around, talking to everyone, and having a good time, but no one told you that you have stuff stuck in your teeth. You know they saw it, but they just didn't have the guts to tell you or they didn't want to embarrass you.

Honest communication in the workplace is the same. It's the same concept. No one wants to walk around with broccoli in his teeth. No one wants to work without the knowledge that you think his interactions with the children could be better or that other members on his team are upset with him. Employees can't improve skills they don't know need improving. We need to tell people about their performance, because if we don't tell them, they won't know. Challenge yourself to communicate consistently and honestly to your employees. Don't you expect the same from them?

What Do You Communicate?

We've established that honest communication is a good thing, but don't run out and tell everyone what you think about them. *I don't like your hair. You can't draw. Is that your husband!?* Before communicating honestly, we have to decide what to communicate and why. So how do we know what information about an employee's performance is valuable to share? Begin by asking yourself this simple question: *Does it really matter?*

Does It Really Matter?

- Does it really matter *that food is all over the floor?*
- Does it really matter *that a teacher is upset with another teacher?*
- Does it really matter *that teachers are huddled in a group chatting on the playground?*
- Does it really matter *that a teacher's clothes are out of style?*

So how do we know if it really matters? Ask this second question: *How does it affect the children?* If a concern affects the children in a negative way or impedes the program quality, it is our responsibility to tell the employee.

being a supervisor

How Does It Affect the Children?

If food is all over the floor, children could slip and fall or eat dirty food from the floor or the food could attract bugs. Does it really matter? How does it affect the children? Food on the floor really matters, and it affects the children in a negative way. Do we tell employees to make sure they get all the food off the floor after meals? You betcha!

How about an individual teacher's clothing style? Does it really matter? Do you have a dress code? Is her clothing clean and neat? Is she able to get on the floor easily with the children? Is she covered up? If the teacher's dress meets the center policies and allows her to do her job, then it doesn't affect the children and it doesn't really matter. Do we tell the teacher to go out and buy some new clothes? No. We might not particularly like her clothing style, but that's just our preference. It doesn't really matter.

Steps to Communicating Honestly

Follow these steps consistently, and you'll be an honest communicator.

1   Make sure your information is accurate. Is there really a situation here, or is it your own or someone else's frustration, annoyance, or personal preference?

2   Observe the situation and document your findings.

3   Consult your supervisor.

4   Ask *Does it really matter?* and *How does it affect the children?*

5   Determine whether there is an issue or concern to communicate.

6   Put the issue or concern in writing. Prepare what you will say and practice before you meet with the employee.

7   Set up a time and a private place to speak with the employee.

8   Bring a colleague for support or as a witness, if necessary.

9   Get to the point. Bring notes for referral.

10   Express how you feel and validate how the person feels or might feel.

11   Be honest. Long-term credibility is more important than short-term unpleasantness.

12   Give an explanation, not an excuse.

13   Expect varied emotional responses from different individuals.

14 Let the person vent. Explain, and contribute to the conversation.

15 Offer the employee ways to help him succeed. Have these ideas and resources written down to hand to the person.

16 End the meeting.

17 Commend yourself for delivering a difficult message.

Communicate as Much Information as Possible

Remember, not all the information that you communicate to your staff will be unfavorable. Most of the communication will be positive and informative. The more information people have about the program and what's happening, the more invested they are in improving quality and having ownership of the program. Let your staff know about your meetings and who is coming to the center. Tell them about center tours, the budget, and ideas for the playground—everything you know that is not confidential. Why? Two reasons: first, information is power, and as a supervisor you have a lot more power. When that information is given to employees, they too have power and knowledge about the program and can feel more involved in the school. Hopefully, as discussed in chapter 3, you will have asked for their input on a variety of these issues and they will have helped to shape the information you are communicating. Second, the absence of information creates a culture of wondering what is happening, speculation, and even gossip. Keep your staff informed.

One way to include staff in the communication process is by using a communication checklist like the one on the following page. Having a documented communication process can be helpful for you and your employees when you're trying to tackle a complicated situation. The process can also give you some necessary steps to double-check before making assumptions about the communication exchange. Use this form as a guide for yourself or make copies of it for others to use and then discuss with you as needed. (It is also available for downloading at www.redleafpress.org.)

being a supervisor

Form 4 Communication Checklist

What I See Happening (Issue or Concern)

_____

_____

_____

What I Want to See Happening (Job Expectation)

_____

_____

_____

Yes ❑ No ❑ **1** I have observed the situation and documented my findings.

Yes ❑ No ❑ **2** I have consulted my supervisor.

Yes ❑ No ❑ **3** I have determined there is an issue because it affects the children.

Yes ❑ No ❑ **4** I have put the issue in writing.

Yes ❑ No ❑ **5** I have set up a time and private place to speak with the employee.

Yes ❑ No ❑ **6** I have prepared what I will say and have practiced before I meet with the employee.

Yes ❑ No ❑ **7** I have written a list of ideas and resources to help the employee succeed and am prepared to give these to the employee.

Yes ❑ No ❑ **8** I have identified a situation in which a person needs help, and I want to help that person.

Ways to Communicate Information

Remember that employee performance issues require an initial face-to-face meeting to discuss the job concern. You can't inform someone of a performance issue via voice mail. That might be easier, but not as effective and certainly not as professional. You can, however, use a variety of the ideas below to follow up a meeting and provide continued support.

Ideas for Communication

* Weekly e-mails or memos of what's happening in the program to keep staff "in the know"

* Weekly recognition of various employees who are doing exceptional things in the center, "in the wow"

* In-person conversations

* E-mails to individuals, small groups, or the entire staff

* Memos

* Voice mail messages

* Video clips

* Regularly scheduled team meetings

* One-on-one meetings

* Posters

* Thought for the day

* Copies of articles

* Copies of e-mails sent to you—if they are not confidential

* Awards

* Performance appraisals (A performance appraisal should never be the first time an employee is hearing about a poor performance issue. Performance issues and concerns should be addressed as they occur.)

being a supervisor

Meetings

Effective meetings can be a great way to share information and encourage employees' ideas and input. Ineffective meetings can dampen or even hinder program quality. Meetings that don't start on time don't allow for the input of others; meetings that cover agenda items that could have been easily put in a memo often make people feel their time was wasted and they could have been doing more productive things in their rooms. Check out the tips below for running and attending meetings to make them more effective for communicating honestly.

Tips for Running an Effective Meeting

- Survey employees to find out the most convenient time to meet. You may not be able to find a time that works well for everyone.

- Give attendees plenty of advance notice. If you schedule a regular weekly or monthly meeting, prepare and distribute a calendar of meetings for the year.

- Limit meetings to an hour if possible.

- Have a start time and an end time so that people cover agenda items efficiently. End early if the agenda is completed.

- Prepare an agenda. Solicit employees for items they may want to include as meeting topics.

- Circulate the agenda in advance so people can think about the issues and be prepared to discuss them.

- Start on time. Employees will come later and later if they know you don't start on time.

- Draw closure to an agenda item when people get off course or have discussed the item for a considerable time. *Let's conclude our comments and list what we are going to do.* Or, *We need to move on. If you have further comments, you can call or e-mail me.*

- If the meeting has many attendees and there is need for further discussion and decision making, form a subgroup to meet individually and report back.

- Produce minutes from the meeting outlining the conclusions the group drew, the plans made, who is responsible, and deadline dates.

Tips for Attending an Effective Meeting

- Arrive on time.

- Listen to the discussion without interrupting others.

- Make your comments clear and brief.

- Avoid summarizing someone else's point.

- Be involved in the discussion. Even if you are shy or uncomfortable, make an effort to speak at least once. Unfortunately, quiet attendees may be viewed as aloof or unconcerned. Besides, you probably have great contributions to make! Speak up.

SELF-ASSESSMENT

How am I Doing "Communicating Honestly"?

How well do you communicate honestly with your staff? Take a look at the questions below and assess yourself and your communication patterns. Be honest with yourself about what you do, not just what you think you should do. Supervisors who are great communicators in one area often can still improve in other areas. Does that sound like you? It certainly is me.

1 I keep my staff aware of what is happening in the center.

Always   Usually   Sometimes   Never

List three ways you inform staff of important information.

1 _____

2 _____

3 _____

Record a few items that you don't communicate to staff on a regular basis but should.

1 _____

2 _____

3 _____

2   I deal with performance issues as they occur.

Always   Usually   Sometimes   Never

What performance issues do you currently need to address? How do you know they really matter? How do they affect the children?

Performance Issue	What's Happening?	What Should Happen?	Does It Really Matter?	How Does It Affect the Children?

3   I feel comfortable delivering difficult messages.

Always   Usually   Sometimes   Never

In what ways do you feel uncomfortable and need more confidence in delivering difficult messages? Review the points on the list titled "Steps to Communicating Honestly" in this chapter, and note the ones that can help you be more successful in your conversations.

_____

_____

_____

4   I run effective meetings.

Always   Usually   Sometimes   Never

How can your meetings be more effective?

_____

_____

_____

winning ways

Communication can either make or break a relationship between a supervisor and employee or even the whole team. You as the leader have a great deal of influence over the consistency and efficacy of communication in your program. You can help your employees be more invested in their work by letting them know as much as possible about what is happening in the center and by listening to their concerns. And then, after you've communicated well, be sure you follow through on your ideas and commitments—the topic of chapter 6. Most of us are high on ideas and low on follow-through. Early childhood programs are busy. How do you make follow-through a priority? Your reputation and effectiveness as a supervisor depend on it.

OPTIMIZE YOUR KNOWLEDGE

1 What are some **barriers** to honest communication?

_____

_____

_____

_____

2 What does it mean to say **information is power**? Explore this idea in a group discussion or on your own.

_____

_____

_____

_____

3 Observe your next meeting, keeping track of things that help the meeting and the group as well as things that don't work. Analyze how you might **change** the meeting next time.

_____

_____

_____

_____

being a supervisor

6

Follow Through

I follow through on the tasks and priorities I've promised for myself and my team.

- Always

- Usually

- Sometimes

- Never

ONE OF JENNA'S GREATEST STRENGTHS *as a supervisor was her ability to connect with her staff. She was always asking for their input, spending time in the classroom, and maintaining an open-door policy. Everyone felt comfortable going to Jenna with their questions and concerns. She was motivating, and people enjoyed hanging out with her.*

Jenna usually made a to-do list each day but rarely accomplished the tasks. She would get started on a project, for example, paperwork, but never finished because of the many interruptions by others. She wouldn't place the supply order, review and return lesson plans, or finish the staff schedule. As much as the staff loved Jenna's laid-back approach, they started to get frustrated with her when there were no paper towels and she never returned the work they gave her.

Jenna was having a hard time balancing the daily flow of the program with following through.

You Can Do It!

Learn to:

- ❑ Realize that following through sets a good example for your employees, raises your credibility, and is essential to excellent job performance.
- ❑ Identify how you use your time and how to set priorities.
- ❑ Have realistic job expectations of yourself and others.
- ❑ Aim for excellence, not for perfection.
- ❑ Use your calendar to organize your time.

Stay Positive! Avoid:

- ❑ Making excuses for not completing work.
- ❑ Setting a work pace that is not sustainable over the long term.
- ❑ Not following through because of daily interruptions.

Make It Happen! Here's How

Following Through Can Be Hard: Do It Anyway

There are times in the ever-changing day of an early childhood professional that we just don't get to everything on our to-do list. Our days are often led by coverage issues and other agenda items we never planned on. Shouldn't staff understand that we can't always follow through? Yes and no. The difficulty exists in that other employees don't always understand, nor should they, the entire scope of our job. You may have a day in which you feel you have followed through by finishing paperwork, dealing with an upset parent, and collecting materials for an unexpected visit from your licensor. Did you work hard? Did you do a lot? Sure, but at the end of that same day, one teacher may feel you didn't follow through because you didn't review her lesson plan for the next week and return it to her as you promised.

In this follow-through situation, the parent and the licensor do take priority, and the teacher can probably understand that, but if you are continually not reviewing her lesson plans on time, then you aren't following through, regardless of the other work you have. Think of it from her point of view. She can't begin preparing for the following week or move forward with her work until she has your approval. Imagine how frustrating that is. So what do you do? Review your expectations. Is it really necessary for you to approve her plans? If so, make it a priority and follow through.

Why Is Following Through So Important?

As a supervisor, following through is important because you can't expect others to do their job, to follow through, if you don't. You are their role model, and role models set the standard of commitment, dedication, and work ethic for their employees. You have an incredible amount of authority and influence over others. Everyone is looking to you, whether you think they are or not. What you do, or don't do, matters.

Think about children again. The way we talk to children and interact with them is far more influential than what we tell them. If we use "please" and "thank you," children will use "please" and "thank you." One of the most accurate ways to see what children are learning from the adults in their lives is to watch the children during dramatic play. If the children are playing school, you'll probably hear them utter the very words you say to them. Sometimes it's funny to see them imitate us, and at other times, it's not so funny, especially when we hear them acting stern or harsh, just as we have.

Reasons Why We Don't Follow Through

- We don't even get started. *There are lots of other things I could do instead.* Sometimes the job is boring or tedious. Will it be less boring or tedious later? No, just get started, and momentum will follow.

- We feel overwhelmed. *There's just too much to do.* Break the task into more manageable pieces and ask for help. Do a little each day.

- We don't know where to start. *Where do I start?* Ask other people to help.

- We're afraid to fail. *What if I mess up?* We're not trying new things and learning if we don't sometimes make a mistake. Often our mistakes or problems lead us to some of our most innovative plans.

- We don't have money in the budget. *I can't do anything until I can afford to spend a little more money on it.* Initiatives don't always require money. Do a toy or manipulative swap at the center. Moving toys and furniture to different rooms will make teachers feel as though they have new equipment and supplies.

- We've never tried this before. *What if it fails?* There's a first time for everything. Consult another teacher or program that has done something similar and ask for some advice.

- **We're not good at that kind of thing.** *We just don't do that here.* We can't organize computer and music classes for the children. Chances are there are teachers in your center who have the skills and talents to do all types of things. You just need to identify those skills, ask them to help, and encourage them to get involved.

- **We don't have time.** *There's way too much going on to focus on something new.* If something is a priority, make time. There is never a good time to start a new project or initiative. Late in the day? Get started anyway; one or two steps get you closer to the goal.

- **We don't think it will work.** *What if we do all that work and nothing comes of it?* Some things won't work, but you'll never know if you don't try. I'm sure people thought cell phones and computers would never work.

- **We're not in the mood.** *I'll be more excited to start this tomorrow.* If you're not in the mood for a particular task, you probably never will be. Just dive in. Take the action, and maybe the mood will follow.

Don't Live in the "As Soon As"

There are lots of reasons why we don't always follow through. It's easy to become overwhelmed, excited, and anxious all at the same time when we think about improving our children's program. Often, we eagerly wait for the day when everything will be "just right"—all the teachers hired, children sitting quietly and learning, compliant parents with completed forms and tuition in hand. When we are working with people, especially children, to build relationships, that day of a perfect program never really comes. Perhaps it's more realistic to learn how to ride the rapids in our children's programs than it is to keep searching for smooth waters or making excuses for why we can't follow through with the work we should or want to do.

Many of us are looking for an "And they all lived happily ever after" day. Is it really possible to live happily ever after as a supervisor in an early childhood program? Yes, it is. It's all a matter of how you learn to cope, prioritize, and work in an environment that's exciting and dynamic. We often think that as soon as we get the new toddler teacher hired, things will be fine. As soon as we get the new classrooms opened, things will be fine. As soon as we get accredited, as soon as we lose ten pounds, as soon as . . .

Stop living in the "as soon as." Whatever your center or classroom is right now, that is what you have to work with. That's the point from which you need to determine the work that needs to be accomplished, to whom to delegate

being a supervisor

that work, what your responsibility is, and how to get it completed well and on time. So can you live happily ever after? Yes, you can. You can even live like Cinderella, but do remember she started out scrubbing floors and doing toilets just like we do.

Priorities: What Do You Spend Your Time Doing?

We all follow through with true priorities. Most of us couldn't start the day without a shower and a cup of coffee. We make it happen because it's a priority in our lives and, in many cases, a habit. Supervisors are typically hardworking people; that's how you got promoted. Many of us are heading over the edge—we have the "over-" syndrome. The "over-" syndrome is about how we tend to get ourselves immersed in too many things in our professional and personal lives. It's being overscheduled, overworked, overcommitted, overtired, and overstressed. Sound like you?

Think about this question: "What are your priorities?" If you took the time to make a list of your work and life priorities, it would be very interesting. And if I asked you, "Are these things you want to accomplish?" you would respond, "Of course, those are my work and life priorities." Now, what if you made a second list, a list of what you actually do in a day or a week? There's no question that the list would be long and impressive. You're a hard worker, and you accomplish much. But if we put the two lists side by side, they would probably look very different. You have a list of what you want to do, and you have a list of what you actually do.

What Are Your True Priorities?

Here's what's interesting: your priorities in work and life are not what you write on a list but what you are actually doing. Here's what I mean by that. If that list is what you are doing, then the list reveals your priorities. Otherwise you would be doing something else.

If one of your priorities on the first list is to lose weight, then the second list should have multiple entries about eating well, exercising, and getting enough sleep. If one of your priorities is hiring a new teacher, then you should have multiple entries on the second list about calling parents for potential employee referrals, putting an ad in the paper, and training teachers so they can be promoted from within. Get the idea? Priorities equal action. What you do is what is important to you.

Don't Make Excuses

Now a lot of people will say, "But I can't accomplish the priority I want to accomplish because of the situation I'm dealing with," or "I can't because this is what is going on with coverage," or "I can't because of ratio issues." Your actions are your priorities. If you want things to be different, you have to change your actions. And you're the only person who can do that. And sometimes that change is really difficult because it means you have to deal with your board or supervisor, your financial resources, your budget, or marginal performing staff members.

Some priorities are ongoing. You might be able to check them off for the day, but they are everyday priorities, like walking through or spending time in the classrooms, having an open-door policy, and making sure you meet ratios. Let me give you another example. I have four children and a husband, and the laundry in my house is not even a pile; it's a mountain. I have to go buy new underwear for everybody because we're running out of it, there's just so much laundry to do. Like you, I'm the kind of person who is task oriented and wants to get everything done. The only way I'm ever going to get all my laundry done is if everybody in my family is naked and all the sheets are stripped off the beds. That's never going to happen.

So look at what you spend your time doing, and if you want to spend it doing something else, do it. If you wish you were organizing something for your school or writing an article to be published, or if you want to do a workshop, make that a priority. And make it happen. Nobody else is going to do it for you. And you have great stuff to share, so you should share it with other people.

Where Does Your Time Go?

Unfortunately, memory is a very poor guide when it comes to assessing how you spend your time. A revealing technique is to keep an activity log for several days. Without modifying your behavior, jot down the things you do as you do them, from the moment you start working. Every time you change activities, whether changing diapers or reading a memo, note it. Is how you are spending your time matching up with your priorities?

What Do You Need to Accomplish? Make a List

Even if the things you want to achieve do not seem overwhelming and you can keep them "in your head," make a written list. To-do lists are extremely useful ways of organizing your time efficiently.

being a supervisor

1　Write down the tasks you must do or want to do each day.

2　If they are complicated tasks, break them down into smaller components.

3　Do this until everything you have to do is listed.

4　Look at each task and allocate priorities from 1 to 5: 1 is very important and 5 is unimportant.

5　If too many tasks have a high priority, run through the list again and demote the less important high-priority items.

6　Once you have done this, rewrite the task list in priority order.

7　You now have a precise list of priorities.

8　You can use the list to eliminate unnecessary or redundant tasks or identify problems.

9　Check off the tasks you complete and enjoy the satisfaction of a job well done.

10　Use the list from the previous day to prepare your new daily list. It's unlikely that you will accomplish everything you want to do in a day, but if you do, way to follow through!

Take Care of Yourself and Business

It's easy to get burned out in early childhood education, especially as a supervisor who has lots of ideas and energy. You also tend to take your work very seriously, which is good as long as you take care of yourself very seriously too. Who is going to take care of you? You have to take care of yourself. Nobody else is going to do it for you.

Think about creative ways you can incorporate your work commitments and taking care of yourself. Ever arrive at the center before daylight and leave after dark? You were there a long time, probably too long. How do you get some fresh air and leave those center walls? If you have a meeting with a staff member, do a walking meeting.

Schedule Time for Yourself

Do you have a calendar? It's a good starting point as a supervisor. But do you really use your calendar to your professional and personal advantage? Imagine you have a meeting with your governing board or supervisor and you have that on the calendar. You check your calendar for the day, and it says, "Meet with the board." Would you just decide, "I don't want to go to that board meeting; I'm going to go get my nails done"? Certainly not, if you want to keep your job. We tend to take the things that are on our calendars very seriously. That's why we put it on the calendar in the first place. You just don't blow it off. If something's on the calendar, you actually do it.

So use your calendar to accomplish your priorities and to make time for yourself. Whatever it is that you are going to do for you to make your life more happily ever after, put it on your calendar; make it a habit. Here's how it works. You want to make sure you actually take time for lunch, so put it on your calendar. Now your calendar should show: Lunch, 12:00 p.m. Suppose someone calls you and asks for a meeting on the same day at the same time. You respond, "Let me check my calendar. You know, I already have a meeting at noon on that day. What other day or time could we meet?" You have a meeting in a park with yourself, eating lunch. Protect your time to renew yourself with lunch while offering an alternative time to meet with the other person.

If there is something important you want to accomplish, put it on your calendar and take it seriously. Write down on your calendar time that you are going to block off for yourself. Maybe you're going to watch a training video or write an article. Perhaps it's as simple as reading one of your early childhood publications. No time to read the articles that may help you do your job better? Put "Read *ECE* magazine, 10:00 a.m." on your calendar. Do that for you, because no one else will.

SELF-ASSESSMENT

How Am I Doing with "Following Through"?

As a busy supervisor, follow through can be easy to say and hard to do. Great supervisors learn how to follow up on their promises to others and also the priorities they set for themselves. How well do you follow through in your daily work? How is your follow-through with long- and short-term goals? Can you really stick with something until it is completed? Take some time to evaluate yourself with the following questions.

1 I follow through with job responsibilities.

    Always   Usually   Sometimes   Never

List tasks that you sometimes do not follow through on or are late in completing.

_____   _____

_____   _____

_____   _____

2 I do not make excuses for not accomplishing my work.

Always   Usually   Sometimes   Never

Review your list above of tasks you don't always complete and write down why you have trouble following through.

_____   _____

_____   _____

_____   _____

3 I spend the majority of my time trying to accomplish my priorities.

Always   Usually   Sometimes   Never

What do you spend the majority of your time doing?

_____

_____

_____

Are the tasks above helping you accomplish your priorities?

_____

_____

_____

What is keeping you from accomplishing your job goals and priorities?

_____

_____

_____

Tips for Handling the "OVER-" Syndrome

OVERSCHEDULED

- Use "routine times," dressing, eating, driving to work as "prime times" to enjoy life.
- Schedule lunch with yourself or an hour with yourself at least once a week.
- Schedule lunch with a friend or family member.
- Schedule an outing each month.
- Schedule an "inning" each month. What's an inning? Make a date to stay home.
- Read, take a walk, play a board game.

OVERCOMMITTED

- Set priorities for your time: family, work, community.
- Only volunteer for or accept additional responsibilities that fit your goals.
- Realize that most pressure to complete tasks is internalized.

OVERWORKED

- Don't procrastinate; complete work as it comes.
- Organize your home and office so you clean as you go; avoid weekend overhauls.
- List all your responsibilities, and eliminate one if possible.
- Ask for help and give help.
- Give others responsibilities.

OVERINDULGED

- Avoid buying too many things; the more you have the more you have to take care of.
- Even if you can afford it, don't buy something every time you go in a store, not even gum.
- Avoid giving yourself too many choices.
- Set limitations.

OVERTIRED

- Put your children to bed on time at the same time every time.
- Put yourself to bed on time; turn off the TV.
- Close your eyes and relax for at least ten minutes; take a nap if possible.
- Avoid quick "pick-me-ups" such as coffee, soda, and carbs.

being a supervisor

OVERSTRESSED

- Realize that you cannot control how others act, but you can control how you react to them; this includes your reaction to your children.

- Be the thermostat, not the thermometer.

- Exercise—it really works.

- Do something for yourself. Don't play "poor, pitiful, hardworking, self-sacrificing me"; no one really wants to hear it.

- Take time to engage in the spiritual aspect of your life.

Following through can be one of the most important things you do as a supervisor, and your employees will love you for it. Employees can trust and depend on supervisors who follow through. Examine your priorities and make sure you do what's important to you and for your program. Then give yourself time and patience for those times you don't do what you said you would—you're learning too, and you'll get it next time! (Or your employees might get you!) How do you maintain a good relationship with your employees? Stay connected. Staying connected to your employees is discussed in chapter 7.

OPTIMIZE YOUR KNOWLEDGE

1 In your words, what does it mean for something to be a **priority**? List three priorities for your program.

1 _____

2 _____

3 _____

2 How effective are **calendars and scheduling** at helping you follow through? What's helpful or not helpful about them?

_____

_____

_____

_____

3 What are your **"over-" syndrome** tendencies? What causes you to overdo your activities? Take some time to analyze your habits and to explore ideas for taking time for yourself.

_____

_____

_____

_____

being a supervisor

7

Stay Connected

I know and connect with each of my employees regularly to give encouragement and to address problems.

- Always
- Usually
- Sometimes
- Never

KEVIN'S TEAM WAS ONE OF THE MOST ORGANIZED *groups of teachers in the center. With the input of his staff, Kevin had clearly outlined the job expectations, and everyone felt comfortable about their roles and performed at a high level of excellence. It was no surprise that families and children wanted that preschool class.*

But halfway through the year, Kevin began spending more time in his office and only showing up in the classroom during center tours or when his supervisor was around. The staff felt distanced from Kevin, and although he was working hard on enrollment and community projects for the center, they felt that he wasn't a part of their team anymore. "He doesn't seem to see our efforts anymore. And we miss him. He really inspired us to work hard and enjoy our jobs."

You Can Do It!

Learn to:

- ❑ Get to know your employees as individuals.
- ❑ Offer employee recognition on a regular basis.
- ❑ Express empathy for the hard work of employees.
- ❑ Deal with problems when they arise.
- ❑ Check in with employees to ask, "How are things going?"

Stay Positive! Avoid:

- ❑ Thinking your responsibilities are more important than what the teachers are doing in the classroom.
- ❑ Missing an opportunity to connect with an employee.
- ❑ Not allowing employees to complain occasionally.

Make It Happen! Here's How

See Every Employee as Important

Child check. When you see a group of children, what do you notice? You'd probably note how they vary, not only in appearance but also in how they take on the world. We might not want to admit it, but we are drawn to certain children. It's not that we don't love them all, but certain ones tend to tug on our hearts, and other children can tug on our patience. But as good teachers, we care for every child and encourage them all to succeed. It's the same with adults, or it should be. There are employees we supervise whom we just feel more comfortable with, and working together is easy. There are others who tend to annoy or irritate us, and sometimes that's not even tied to job performance. We might like the company of a marginal performer and feel put off by the overachiever. Either way, it's your responsibility to stay connected to each employee and recognize his or her contributions.

How can you do it? It's hard, and that's why we have the primary caregiving system for children, to make sure no one falls through the cracks, that each child gets time and attention. Do we need a primary caregiving system for adults? Kind of. You have to ensure that each employee receives adequate time and attention from you. That doesn't mean that adults are children and everyone gets equal time. On the contrary, it means that you stay connected to your employees enough to know who needs help, how you can support them, and how you recognize their efforts. Use your influence and power to encourage others, even those who irritate you just a bit.

Why Is Staying Connected Important?

Most of us in early childhood education don't work for a large amount of money. That's no surprise. So why do we show up every day? The children are one reason, of course, and another is that people like the sense of belonging that comes from working with a group and the satisfaction of a job well done. That's where you, as the supervisor, come in. Staying connected to your staff and cultivating that feeling of belonging is part of your job. You can be the type of supervisor who knows her employees, takes an interest in their ideas, and recognizes their efforts—efforts of success and efforts of just giving it a try. Or you can be the type of supervisor who hides out in her office "working," rushes through as she travels from meeting to meeting, or even sees herself as a bit above the rest of the crew with a "no time to get my hands dirty" attitude. Which type of supervisor would you want to work for?

SELF-ASSESSMENT

A Quick Checklist about Staying Connected: How Do I Rate?

Your job is more than that one difficult employee or busy schedule. It includes balancing the daily routine with the unexpected and, in early childhood, there can be lots of unexpecteds. In the midst of your crazy schedule, how do you take time to connect and build relationships with all your staff? Knowing each staff member who directly reports to you is essential to your success as a supervisor. Look at the following statements and think about your style of supervising and connecting. Are you a relational person? You need to be.

1 I provide opportunities to connect with my staff that are convenient for them.

Always   Usually   Sometimes   Never

2 I provide support to my staff in a manner that seems timely to them.

Always   Usually   Sometimes   Never

3 I create a welcoming and safe environment for my staff.

Always   Usually   Sometimes   Never

4 I create a welcoming and safe environment for my staff.

Always   Usually   Sometimes   Never

5 I am respectful and polite to staff even when they are rude and demanding.

Always   Usually   Sometimes   Never

6 I care for each employee as an individual.

Always   Usually   Sometimes   Never

7 I am compassionate about the professional and personal circumstances of each employee.

Always   Usually   Sometimes   Never

8 I treat all employees as partners and involve them in decisions about the work we are doing.

Always   Usually   Sometimes   Never

9 When I provide help, I do so in a way that is sensitive to the employee's personal preference and cultural and ethnic background.

Always   Usually   Sometimes   Never

10 I am professional with staff at all times regardless of the circumstances.

Always   Usually   Sometimes   Never

Affirm Employees' Efforts: The Importance of Supervisory Praise

Try this quick exercise.

1 Find something to write with and a piece of something to write on. Anything will do.

2 Think of the staff member whom you do not connect with easily.

3 Recall something she did recently that was commendable.

4 Give yourself sixty seconds, just one minute, to write that employee a note of affirmation.

5 Sign your name to the note and give it to the employee.

being a supervisor

Here are some examples:

Dear Beca, I was impressed with how you jumped in to offer coverage for the other classroom without being asked. Thank you, Natasha

Dear Jonathan, You did a tremendous job organizing the supply closet. I appreciate what you did. Many thanks, Robin

Dear Trang, Wow! You're so creative. I love the way you arranged the dramatic play area like a restaurant. The children will love it. — Kayla

Dear _____,
I really appreciate the way you
_____
Many thanks, _____

The example notes are simple, specific, and quick. It took only sixty seconds or less to write each one. But are they really meaningful? When someone gives you a letter of affirmation, what do you do? Imagine that one of your employees left a sticky note in your box, saying, *Last night's staff meeting was really fun. Thank you for going to all the trouble.* Would you crumple up the paper and toss it in the trash? Never! It doesn't matter that it was written on a sticky note; the note still made you feel good and helped you realize that others do appreciate your work. If somebody leaves you a voice mail affirming your job performance, you don't erase it immediately; you listen to it over and over. Notes, e-mails, voice mails, and verbal comments that recognize our efforts make us feel good about the job we do and motivate us to continue.

Take Time to Recognize Employees

Affirmation and recognition are important. How long did it take to write that note? It took sixty seconds. Many of us walk around our center and notice staff members doing really positive things, and then we usually make a mental note. And we think things like, "You know what I'm going to do for that employee? I'm going to go out and get him a gift card. Oh no, I'm going to get him balloons. Oh no, I'm going to bake cupcakes. I'm going to make cookies. I'm going to bake a ham. I'm going to wash his car." Our intentions of letting staff know they are doing a good job are positively directed. But what usually happens? Nothing. We never recognize the employee because we never got the right card or the perfect present. Sure, it's good to show people our affirmation in professional and creative ways, but don't abandon the sentiment merely because you didn't have the right card. Do you think an employee would rather have a note from you on a scrap piece of paper or no note at all because you never got to the card store?

The point of this exercise is that you can notice, recognize, and motivate an employee in sixty seconds using a scrap of paper. Do you have a scrap of paper? Do you have a minute? If you only write one note a week—that's sixty seconds a week—you will give encouragement fifty-two times a year. What a difference that could make. More important, what a difference *you* could make.

28 Ways to Stay Connected to Your Staff and Recognize Their Efforts

1 Put little notes in their center mailboxes, on their cars, or in their classrooms.

2 Tuck small treats in their mailboxes or classrooms, like candy, cards, books, lotion, or gift cards.

3 Tell the employees, verbally, in front of other people, how wonderful they are.

4 Write letters of commendation and copy them to your supervisor and senior administrators.

5 Create "of the week" or "of the month" awards, like greatest activity with the children, funniest moment, or amazing effort.

6 Have a party at your home during the holidays and dress up, or invite the employees and their families for a picnic in the park.

being a supervisor

7   Have a lottery and award an extra break, double lunch, or pass on paperwork.

8   Include regular weekly or monthly recognition at staff meetings. Put it on the agenda.

9   Give employees leadership opportunities.

10 Observe and make notes about how each person likes to be recognized individually. What are staff members' hobbies? What kinds of foods do they each like?

11 Send a letter to an employee's home.

12 Have an employee appreciation day or week and get families involved.

13 Tell families and other program leaders how amazing individuals are on your staff.

14 Make them take their paid days off.

15 Go to their meetings. Let them know you'll be coming.

16 Put posters of recognition in the lobby for everyone to see.

17 Celebrate everyone's birthday.

18 Be more obvious about taking a serious interest in employees as individuals.

19 Follow up with them about questions, issues, or ideas.

20 Surprise your employees with a lunch, a teacher field trip, or new supplies.

21 Put little coupons for lunch together in their mailbox.

22 Have them contribute to staff meeting agendas.

23 Leave positive notes in their workspaces.

24 Decorate their doors for no reason.

25 Make or buy treats for your staff. Leave a little note.

26 Keep a success jar in your office and make a point of filling it with employees' successes.

27 Read the successes at staff meetings.

28 Have your supervisor call employees who have done something great.

Offer Empathy

Working in a service industry like early childhood education can be physically and emotionally demanding. In addition, we work hard to create a familylike, relationship-focused environment. When we deal with relationships, we deal with feelings. Sometimes we're excited about what's happening in the program, and at other times, we may be frustrated or upset. It's okay to be upset—it's how we express our frustration that matters. It's not okay to be unprofessional, to speak inappropriately in front of the parents or children, or to be unable to move beyond the emotional state.

Often when an employee is upset, she just wants to be heard. She may not even need your advice. She may just need your empathy and an affirmation that you understand what she does every day and that it's a difficult and challenging job. You understand that only a special kind of person can work in early childhood education.

Ever feel like that yourself? You just want your supervisor to say, "I know. I've been there. It's tough." When someone else has an understanding of our situation, we feel more motivated to stick it out, to make it work. We're not talking about continually offering empathy to chronic complainers, those who always seem to be a little upset. But for the once-in-a-while complainers, listening to them, allowing them to vent in a safe place, and offering empathy will help them defuse and get back out there. Empathy should help productivity.

The 2 Percent Rule

Here's a rule you might find interesting. It's called the 2 Percent Rule. It states that 2 percent of the population is difficult to help, often chronic complainers, so no matter what we do, they're never pleased. Those particular people make our jobs in early childhood education difficult. Those 2 percent are likely to exhibit the same complaining pattern of behavior at the dry cleaners, at restaurants, with their in-laws, and at the doctor's office. It's probably just habit.

Are you thinking the statistics should be higher, that the world is full of unhappy people? Maybe, but I hope not. I made up the 2 Percent Rule, so there's actually no research behind the rule, just an optimistic person who thinks the majority of people want to succeed.

So do we just give up on that 2 percent? Absolutely not. Regardless of how others act or how we think they will act, we continue to do what is right. Who knows, maybe those 2 percent complain more because no one has ever really listened to them and offered them a little empathy. Maybe there would be no 2 Percent Rule if everyone felt a little support. Offer empathy and support when you can.

being a supervisor

Address Problems and Build Employee Relationships

As a supervisor, if you have a complainer whom you've listened to and supported, and things haven't gotten better, then what you really have is a performance issue. Constant complainers, gossipers, and those with a bad attitude can quickly tear down your team and the morale. They tear the team down in many ways by:

- Making others think there is a problem when there is not.
- Creating doubt in others.
- Undermining your credibility when you fail to address the issue or take action.
- Spreading the issue: a bad attitude can be contagious.

Address problems and you will build employee relationships and trust. A gift card is not as motivating to an employee as a supervisor who deals with issues and protects the team.

How to Address Problems

Don't fear problems. We will all have many. You will build some of your greatest relationships with staff, families, the community, and everyone you come in contact with when you deal with a problem well. A problem is an opportunity to connect with staff in a deeper and more intimate way. What are you going to do when a problem arises? Deal with the specific concern, but stay connected and follow up. You're going to do four things:

1 Deal with the situation right away. Acknowledge that the person is angry or upset. It doesn't mean that this is the time you have to sit down and talk to him. He may be so angry that you say, *It seems like you are really upset right now. May we meet tomorrow morning to talk about it?* By talking to the person immediately, you dealt with the situation right away.

2 Call or talk to the person the next day or after you have your meeting with him. This is the follow-up piece. *Thank you for meeting with me. I'm just calling to see how things are going and if there is anything else you wanted to add.*

3 Follow up again in a week. Just call and see how things are going with the solution or decision you reached. *How is it going now with the new sick time policy? Are we having fewer unplanned absences from staff?* Put the follow-up on your calendar so you don't forget.

4   Follow up in a couple of months. Again, put a date on your calendar
to call. *How's everything going?* The person will be very surprised and
likely very satisfied that you would call a couple of months later
to see how things are going. You're dealing with the issues, staying
connected, and building relationships. Now, *that's* multitasking.

SELF-ASSESSMENT

How Am I Doing "Staying Connected"?

How well do you connect with your staff? You might struggle to make time
to connect, or perhaps you have difficulty spending time with others because
you are such a doer. Intentionally developing relationships with your staff
members needs a place at the top of your to-do list. Take a look at the statements below and think about your style of supervising specifically regarding
staying connected with staff. You will have some strengths and some areas for
improvement. Try to be honest about both.

1   I see every employee as a capable individual.

   Always   Usually   Sometimes   Never

   Think of an employee with whom you have a hard time connecting.
   List some of the ways you could reach out to her to build a stronger
   relationship.

   _____

   _____

   _____

2   I take time to recognize my employees' successes and efforts to succeed.

Always   Usually   Sometimes   Never

Write down several of the ways in which you are currently recognizing staff.

_____

_____

_____

_____

_____

_____

3   I address problems as they occur.

Always   Usually   Sometimes   Never

What problems have you been avoiding?

_____

_____

_____

4   I follow up with and stay connected to employees who have expressed a concern.

Always   Usually   Sometimes   Never

Name a situation that you should follow up on. Write the dates in your calendar to stay connected a week later and a few months later.

_____

_____

_____

Use the following form for a staff meeting or workshop to stay more connected to your team. It can be photocopied or downloaded from the *Being a Supervisor* page at www.redleafpress.org. Have the participants fill out the form to learn more about how your employees are feeling. Playing a game like this and collecting items that represent their thoughts often makes it easier for people to express themselves. Often when we ask employees, "How are things going?" they respond, "Fine." Good supervisors want to hear more than "fine."

winning ways

Center Scavenger Hunt

Look through the center to find and bring back an item that represents the following statements about your work and experience in the program:

1   I work at the center because . . .

2   The most amazing part of my job is . . .

3   The most demanding part of my job is . . .

4   The last six months have been . . .

5   Here's what I really want to change . . .

being a supervisor

With the many aspects of your program, there's always a lot going on for you to do and supervise. Staying connected with employees will help you supervise better and will create a work culture that is more proactive than reactive, plus staying connected will be a lot more fun for everyone! The supervisor who takes the time to get to know his staff and acknowledge excellent work, not just problems, will guide his employees toward being a great team. Isn't that what you want? And think how good it feels when your supervisor connects with you. But what do your employees get when they connect with you? Are you frantic and hurried or relaxed but driven? As the supervisor, you set the tone for the whole program. What type of feel are you setting? Check out chapter 8 for more information.

OPTIMIZE YOUR KNOWLEDGE

1 How do you show your employees you **appreciate** them? What makes you most feel valued by others—perhaps notes, gifts, or something else?

_____

_____

_____

_____

winning ways

2   What do you think about the idea that conflicts are **opportunities** to connect with staff in deeper ways? Explain your thoughts.

_____

_____

_____

_____

3   Refer to the list "28 Ways to Stay Connected to Your Staff and Recognize Their Efforts." Check the ways you've recognized others in the past, and then circle three ways you will use to **connect** with your staff in the future.

8

Set the Tone

I set a positive, approachable tone for the rest of my staff.

- Always
- Usually
- Sometimes
- Never

MARGIE HAD A CAN-DO ATTITUDE *that really inspired the members of her team. Her to-do list was always ambitious, but staff knew that she would slowly tackle each item on the list until everything was completed. Margie was deliberate and consistent. Her laid-back approach to tackling the work put staff at ease.*

Margie dealt with the daily ups and downs of early childhood education, a lost pacifier or coverage to work out in the afternoon. But when families complained or even questioned anything, Margie would get really upset. Right away, she'd look for someone to blame: "Why didn't that parent know about the field trip? Weren't you supposed to tell her?" "Why didn't you wake that toddler up? Isn't that what the grandmother asked?"

At first her team just tried to make everything perfect so no family member would make comments, but that was impossible. Families always have questions. Then Margie's staff started hiding the family issues from her. It was easier to deal with the concerns themselves than get Margie upset.

You Can Do It!

Learn to:

- ❏ Enjoy your job and have fun.
- ❏ Appreciate your successes and those of your staff.
- ❏ Accept that there will always be issues to work through.

Stay Positive! Avoid:

- ❏ Thinking a professional is only serious and strict.
- ❏ Always moving to the next goal without taking time to celebrate the present positives.
- ❏ Getting flustered when problems arise.

Make It Happen! Here's How

Set the Tone of Your Work Environment

Who sets the tone, the feeling you get when you walk into your center or classroom? You do. As a leader, your attitude sets the tone of the environment. Are you hurried and frantic, or are you tenacious but relaxed? Whom would you rather work for?

Yes, staff, families, and children will have a positive or negative experience based primarily on the person with whom they interact, but how that employee acts depends largely on you—the people you hire, the expectations you have, the freedom for people to be creative, and the way you handle yourself.

What Makes a Genuine Work Atmosphere?

Do you smile, laugh, and have fun at your job? If not, you probably need a new job. Sound harsh? Not really. Can you think of another profession in which it would be more important to be happy than working with young children? Children deserve the type of care and education that comes from people who avoid sarcasm, complaining, and rudeness. Regardless of your age, no one really wants to be around people like that.

Now smiling, laughing, and having fun doesn't mean that every day will be without issue and you'll always be at your best, but it does mean that the majority of time you like what you are doing. Some of us aren't big smilers, and maybe jokes don't come easily. I'm not asking you to be something you aren't. I am asking you to be a supervisor who is passionate about teaching children and adults.

Think about children. Notice how children smile spontaneously, find delight in simple things, and move from crying to laughing in a matter of seconds? That's what we're looking for—honest, real people who enjoy working together.

Be Happy

Did you realize that being happy isn't something you get from other people or things? Other people and things don't make you happy; you do. Being happy is a choice you make. You can choose to be happy or unhappy depending on the circumstances around you. The circumstances may not change, but you can change how you react to them.

It's kind of like the "as soon as" syndrome from chapter 6. As soon as I hire a new teacher, I'll be happy. As soon as I collect the tuition, I'll be happy. As soon as staff members get more training, I'll be happy. Hiring new teachers, collecting tuition, and offering more training are all good things, but you can be happy in the process of doing those jobs. Don't wait for the end result of a task to determine your happiness. You have to complete the tasks anyway, so why not enjoy your work and set a positive tone in your program?

Set a Positive Tone

Do all programs with a positive tone feel the same? No, every center and classroom is going to feel different, even those within the same company. Like I said, your job is to set a positive tone based on the goals of your program and your personality and temperament. If you're organized and detailed oriented, you'll expect that from your staff. If you prefer organized chaos and are more flexible, you'll expect the same. Either way is okay.

What Does Positive Look Like?

I asked a group of teachers to describe what attributes helped to convey a positive or negative experience in other customer service industries, like a hospital or bank. What we do in early childhood education is unique, and we can't really compare ourselves to another profession, but the knowledge of what helps people feel welcome, listened to, and comfortable in other settings can certainly offer assistance.

Take a look at the following lists of negative attributes and check any that may also apply to your program.

GROCERY STORE,
NEGATIVE ATTRIBUTES

___ Loud
___ Crowded
___ Not efficient
___ Expensive
___ Unorganized
___ Poor maintenance
___ Poor customer service
___ Equipment failure
___ Understaffed

MEDICAL CLINIC,
NEGATIVE ATTRIBUTES

___ Feel ignored
___ Wait forever
___ No answers
___ Lack of trust
___ Expensive
___ Crowded
___ Grouchy people
___ No explanations

UNIVERSITY REGISTRAR,
NEGATIVE ATTRIBUTES

___ More concerned about their time than yours
___ Rude
___ Refer you to other departments
___ Inconvenient hours
___ Unreliable
___ Long waits
___ No accountability
___ Automated services

Spend a few minutes looking at the words you checked and consider why you think those things are happening at your program. What can you do to change them?

Now take a look at characteristics that lead to creating a positive environment, setting a good tone. Again, check the ones in which you excel. For the ones that you don't check, how can you make that happen in your center or classroom?

HAIR SALON,
POSITIVE ATTRIBUTES

___ Attractive atmosphere
___ Attentiveness
___ Accommodating
___ Talented professionals
___ Soothing
___ Quality products
___ Positive imaging
___ Positive feedback
___ Get what you pay for

INSURANCE COMPANY,
POSITIVE ATTRIBUTES

___ Personable
___ Knowledgeable
___ No worries
___ Friendly
___ Saves us money
___ Reasonable
___ Good explanations
___ Answered every question

DISNEY WORLD,
POSITIVE ATTRIBUTES

___ Friendly
___ Smiling employees
___ Clean
___ Fun
___ Accommodating
___ Family oriented
___ Safe

being a supervisor

Personality Plus Expectations

Having an easygoing personality and enjoying your job are only the start to creating a positive tone. Smiling and having fun will only get you so far if you never do the work. It's one thing to be happy, but you have to accomplish the goals at the same time. Laughing all the time but not having proper coverage will not create a positive feeling. As you read in chapter 1, demonstrated, consistent performance is essential to creating and sustaining the tone you want.

We have to provide a safe and educational environment for children and adults. Do that with a smile and relaxed attitude, and the quality of your program is likely to increase. Bottom line, do your job well and enjoy doing it.

When You Think Others Are Rude and Ridiculous

There are always going to be demanding parents and employees. Remember the 2 Percent Rule in chapter 7? But even for the people who aren't in the so-called 2 percent, shouldn't we expect them to be demanding? Questions, suggestions, and issues put a blip in our otherwise "try to be happy" days, but questions cause us to stretch and grow in ways we might not have. And that's good for children because it forces us to continually evaluate and improve our program.

Why Should You Even Have to Deal With People Like That?

Just because someone questions your authority doesn't mean you are a bad supervisor or person. Try not to be defensive when others question you. We tend to take things personally. You can set a good tone if you:

- Expect people to have concerns.
- Try to hear the person's true message, despite the delivery.
- Realize that hearing concerns and acting on them makes your program better for children.
- Know that dealing with demanding people is part of the job you are paid to do.
- Have a goal to help all people.
- Understand that angry and rude people often feel a lack of control and/or self-worth.
- Do not let other people's behavior affect how you behave.
- Treat people respectfully despite how they treat you. Why? Because it is the right thing to do.

8 Steps to Confront and Handle Demanding Situations and Difficult People

1 Defuse anger and irritation.

- Let the person talk without you interrupting.
- Say back to the person what you understand he or she said.
- Realize that dealing with difficulty is part of your job.

2 Offer empathy to other people's issues.

- Try not to judge the significance of the complaint or issue.
- Validate the person's feelings of concern.

3 Try to make the people your allies, not your enemies.

- Ask the person to give you his or her ideas for a solution.
- Realize that in almost every complaint there is a legitimate issue.
- Give each person individual, personal attention.

4 Deal with your own frustration and stress.

- Are your job expectations realistic?
- Do you want things your way?
- Are you looking for affirmation and approval from everyone?

5 Focus on the problem, not the people.

- Avoid blaming someone.
- Admit it if you were wrong.
- Give the other person the benefit of the doubt.
- Don't assume people will always respond the same way.

6 Stay calm and confident when you feel pressured.

- Anticipate and prepare for situations.
- Write down what you will do.
- Take a break. Don't be afraid to fail.
- Smile and do your best.

being a supervisor

7 Deal with the situation.

- Is there really a situation, or is it my frustration?
- Ask the advice of another person.
- Document the occasions if necessary.

8 Validate your efforts.

- Realize that dealing with difficult people is challenging.
- Learn from the experience.
- Did you do your best?

Celebrate Successes and Keep an Eye on Future Goals

Do you celebrate the successes of your program while keeping a clear eye on future goals? Most of us probably keep trying to make things better, but do we ever pause to celebrate the work we have done? We know that childhood is a journey, not a race. And becoming a good supervisor is also a journey, not a race. So why do so many of us want to win the race at the expense of the journey?

Think about distributing an annual parent survey for your center. The results are in, and here are a few things to consider. After a year of working hard and motivating your staff, you have received an 80 percent performance approval. How do you feel about that? *Not so good. I don't want to be 80 percent.* Okay, how about 90 percent? How are you feeling about that? *Better, but still not so good.* Try this score, 99.9 percent, almost perfect. So what are you going to do when you receive 99.9 percent? You're going to go through that survey and find that .1 percent where you need improvement. Do we celebrate the 99.9 percent? Eventually, but most of us will check for what we did wrong. That's human nature.

Keep the Glass Half Full

Let's try to reverse our thinking a bit. Even with 80 percent, we can celebrate our successes and still think of ways to do that 20 percent better. Don't we always talk about celebrating the developmental milestones of children, not pushing them to the next level? Can we do that for ourselves too?

Take ten seconds right now and record something you did really well this year. It might have been coaching a teacher or working better with your board or updating the playground. Whatever it was, it needed to be done and you did it. Give yourself a pat on the back and allow your staff to appreciate their successes as well. We can name many more successes than failures, but we tend to focus on our failures instead of our successes. Successes make us feel good and set a positive tone. Note a success or two in the box.

What I accomplished for the program that was really great:

_____

_____

_____

_____

SELF-ASSESSMENT

How Am I Doing "Setting a Positive Tone"?

What you do—or don't do—can set a positive tone in your program. Think about how your employees interact with you and each other. How might you as a supervisor influence that atmosphere in a more positive way? Take a look at the questions below and evaluate yourself honestly.

1 I set a positive tone in my program.

Always   Usually   Sometimes   Never

If your employees were to describe you as a supervisor, what positive attributes would they list? Record them below.

_____

_____

_____

_____

If your employees were to describe you as a supervisor, what negative attributes would they list? Sometimes we can use our positive personality traits in negative ways. Record them below.

_____

_____

_____

_____

being a supervisor

2 I am happy no matter what the circumstances are around me.

Always   Usually   Sometimes   Never

Describe a difficult situation you handled in a positive way.

_____

_____

_____

_____

3 I have clear expectations about the quality of the program.

Always   Usually   Sometimes   Never

What are some of those quality expectations you have? Take a look at the positive attributes listed in this chapter.

_____

_____

_____

_____

4 I deal with demanding people effectively.

Always   Usually   Sometimes   Never

Describe a recent concern someone had about your program and how dealing with that concern improved the care for children.

_____

_____

_____

_____

winning ways

Adults, just like children, often take cues from their environment—if it's peaceful and happy, they're more likely to be peaceful and happy too. If it's grouchy and out of control, they'll be tempted to add to the chaos. The challenge for adults is to recognize their feelings and choose to feel differently, to change the environment so they can be professional and productive. As supervisors, we set much of the work atmosphere and climate for our employees. Creating a positive atmosphere will go a long way toward helping employees enjoy their jobs, communicate well, and ultimately serve children better. And that's what every great supervisor is aiming for.

OPTIMIZE YOUR KNOWLEDGE

1 Two nearly identical programs with a **positive tone** can look very different. What are some things you would expect to find in both programs, regardless of leaders' personalities?

_____

_____

_____

_____

2 How do you tend to respond when people ask questions, present concerns, or offer challenges to your authority? Are there things you could do differently to be more **professional and positive**?

_____

_____

_____

_____

3 List some successes for you and your program that you could **celebrate**, and then brainstorm some creative ways to celebrate. List them here.

_____

_____

_____

_____

being a supervisor

For All You Do

Many of us never even thought about being a supervisor when we began teaching. I didn't. But being a supervisor and guiding and helping adults to succeed can be just as rewarding as working with children, because good supervisors are really just teachers of adults. If you approach the adults you oversee with the same empathy, understanding, and patience you have with young children, most of your employees will succeed—often far beyond your expectations. Are you willing to meet every employee where she or he is? Are you willing to believe that most adults can succeed in early childhood education? Are you willing to let others grow and learn in their own way?

I think you are! Now, be the best supervisor you can be.

Certificate of Achievement

This certificate is presented to

_____

for completing the professional development program:

Winning Ways for Early Childhood Professionals: Being a Supervisor

Gigi L Schweikert

Redleaf Press®
www.redleafpress.org
800-423-8309

Gigi Schweikert
www.gigischweikert.com